PowerShell a
Beginner to Advanced

Part of Micro Learning | PowerShell series - Book No. 3.

Preface

Welcome to "PowerShell and JSON: From Beginner to Advanced." This book is designed to be your comprehensive guide to understanding and mastering the use of JSON within PowerShell, one of the most powerful scripting environments available today.

Why This Book?

As the world of IT and development continues to evolve, the need for robust, efficient, and flexible scripting solutions has never been more critical. PowerShell, with its extensive capabilities and cross-platform support, has emerged as a leading tool for administrators, developers, and IT professionals. JSON (JavaScript Object Notation), on the other hand, has become the ubiquitous format for data interchange, thanks to its simplicity and readability. Combining these two powerful technologies can open up a myriad of possibilities for automation, configuration management, and data manipulation.

Who Is This Book For?

This book is crafted for a broad audience:

- **Beginners**: If you're new to PowerShell or JSON, this book will guide you step-by-step, starting with the basics and gradually moving to more complex concepts. Each chapter builds on the previous one, ensuring a smooth learning curve.

- **Intermediate Users**: If you have some experience with PowerShell or JSON but want to deepen your understanding and expand your skill set, the intermediate sections will help you enhance your proficiency with practical examples and advanced techniques.

- **Advanced Users**: For seasoned PowerShell scripters and developers, the advanced chapters delve into sophisticated topics such as dynamic JSON processing, performance optimization, and integrating JSON with complex systems. Real-world use cases and advanced scripting examples will challenge and inspire you.

What Will You Learn?

Throughout this book, you will:

- Understand the fundamental concepts of PowerShell and JSON.

- Learn how to parse, create, and manipulate JSON data using PowerShell.

- Explore advanced JSON manipulation techniques for handling complex data structures.

- Discover how to integrate JSON with external services and APIs, automating various tasks and workflows.

- Gain insights into performance optimization, troubleshooting, and best practices for handling JSON in PowerShell.

- Apply your knowledge through real-world use cases and practical examples.

Structure of the Book

The book is organized into nine chapters, each focusing on a specific aspect of PowerShell and JSON. The initial chapters lay a solid foundation, while the later chapters cover advanced topics and real-world applications. Appendices provide additional resources, references, and example scripts to support your learning journey.

A Note of Encouragement

Whether you're embarking on your scripting journey or seeking to elevate your skills to new heights, this book is designed to be a reliable companion. The combination of PowerShell and JSON can significantly enhance your scripting capabilities, enabling you to tackle a wide range of tasks with confidence and efficiency.

We hope that this book not only equips you with the knowledge and skills you need but also inspires you to explore the vast potential of PowerShell and JSON. Happy scripting!

Thank you for choosing "PowerShell and JSON: From Beginner to Advanced." Let's dive in and start this exciting journey together!

László Bocsó *(Microsoft Certified Trainer - MCT)*

2024

Table of Contents

Chapter 1: Introduction to PowerShell and JSON

Welcome to the first chapter of "PowerShell and JSON: From Beginner to Advanced." This chapter will introduce you to the basics of PowerShell and JSON, laying the groundwork for the more advanced topics covered later in the book. You'll learn what PowerShell and JSON are, why they are important, and how they can be used together.

1.1 What is PowerShell?

PowerShell is a task automation and configuration management framework from Microsoft, consisting of a command-line shell and the associated scripting language. It is built on the .NET framework and provides a powerful tool for system administrators and developers to automate tasks and manage configurations.

Key Points:

- **History of PowerShell**: Introduced in 2006, PowerShell has evolved significantly over the years. Initially designed for Windows, it is now cross-platform, running on Windows, macOS, and Linux.
- **PowerShell Core vs. Windows PowerShell**: Windows PowerShell is the original version, while PowerShell Core is the cross-platform version,

known as PowerShell 7. PowerShell Core has many enhancements and improvements over Windows PowerShell.

Practice:

- **Installing PowerShell:**
    - Windows: Open a command prompt and type powershell.
    - macOS/Linux: Install via package managers like Homebrew (`brew install --cask powershell`) or apt (`sudo apt-get install powershell`).
- **Running Basic Commands:**
    - Open PowerShell and run simple commands like `Get-Process`, `Get-Service`, and `Get-Command`.

1.2 What is JSON?

JSON (JavaScript Object Notation) is a lightweight data interchange format that is easy for humans to read and write and easy for machines to parse and generate. It is widely used for transmitting data in web applications.

Key Points:

- **JSON Structure**: JSON is built on two structures:
    - A collection of key/value pairs (often referred to as an object).
    - An ordered list of values (often referred to as an array).

- **Use Cases of JSON**: Commonly used for APIs, configuration files, and data storage due to its simplicity and flexibility.

Practice:

- **Creating a JSON Object:**
    - Write a simple JSON object in a text editor:

    ```
    {
      "name": "John Doe",
      "age": 30,
      "email": "john.doe@example.com"
    }
    ```

- **Validating JSON:**
    - Use an online JSON validator to check if your JSON object is valid.

1.3 Why Use JSON with PowerShell?

PowerShell and JSON together form a powerful combination for managing data and automating tasks. PowerShell's ability to easily parse and generate JSON makes it a preferred tool for interacting with web APIs and configuration files.

Key Points:

- **Data Interchange Format**: JSON is language-agnostic and widely adopted for data interchange between different systems.
- **Integration with APIs**: Most modern web APIs use JSON for request and response payloads, making PowerShell an ideal tool for automation tasks involving APIs.
- **Configuration Management**: JSON is often used for configuration files due to its readability and ease of use.

Practice:

- **Parsing JSON in PowerShell:**
  - Use `ConvertFrom-Json` to parse a JSON string:

    ```
    $json = '{"name": "Jane Doe", "age": 25, "email":
    "jane.doe@example.com"}'
    $parsedJson = $json | ConvertFrom-Json
    $parsedJson.name
    ```

- **Creating JSON in PowerShell:**
  - Use `ConvertTo-Json` to create a JSON string from a Power-Shell object:

    ```
    $user = @{
       name = "John Smith"
       age = 40
       email = "john.smith@example.com"
    }
    $json = $user | ConvertTo-Json
    $json
    ```

Quiz

1. What is PowerShell, and why is it useful?

   PowerShell is a cross-platform task automation and configuration management framework from Microsoft. It consists of a command-line shell and associated scripting language built on the .NET framework. PowerShell is useful for several reasons:

   - **Automation**: It can automate repetitive tasks and system administration processes.
   - **Flexibility**: It works with various data formats (like JSON, CSV, XML) and can interact with different technologies.
   - **Object-oriented**: Unlike traditional shells that work with text, PowerShell works with .NET objects, allowing for more complex data manipulation.
   - **Extensibility**: It can use .NET libraries and custom modules to extend its capabilities.
   - **Cross-platform**: It runs on Windows, macOS, and Linux.

2. Describe the basic structure of a JSON object.

   A JSON (JavaScript Object Notation) object has the following basic structure:

   - It starts and ends with curly braces { }
   - It contains key-value pairs separated by commas
   - Keys are strings enclosed in double quotes

- Values can be strings, numbers, booleans, null, arrays, or nested objects

```
{
  "name": "John Doe",
  "age": 30,
  "isStudent": false,
  "hobbies": ["reading", "swimming"],
  "address": {
  "street": "123 Main St",
  "city": "Anytown"
  }
}
```

3. How can you convert a JSON string to a PowerShell object?

In PowerShell, you can convert a JSON string to a PowerShell object using the `ConvertFrom-Json` cmdlet. Here's an example:

```
$jsonString = '{"name": "John Doe", "age": 30}'
$psObject = $jsonString | ConvertFrom-Json
```

After conversion, you can access the properties of the object like this:

```
$psObject.name   # Output: John Doe
$psObject.age    # Output: 30
```

4. What are some common use cases for JSON?

JSON is widely used in various scenarios due to its simplicity and readability. Some common use cases include:

- API Communication: Many web APIs use JSON for data exchange between client and server.
- Configuration Files: Applications often use JSON files to store configuration settings.
- Data Storage: JSON is used as a data format in document-oriented databases like MongoDB.

- Cross-language Data Exchange: JSON is language-independent, making it ideal for sharing data between different programming languages.
- Web Development: JSON is commonly used for storing and transporting data in web applications, especially with JavaScript.
- Mobile App Development: JSON is often used for data exchange between mobile apps and backend servers.
- Logging: Some logging systems use JSON format for structured logging.
- Data Export/Import: JSON is a popular format for exporting and importing data between different systems or applications.

These use cases leverage JSON's lightweight nature, easy readability for humans, and straightforward parsing for machines.

In this chapter, you learned about the basics of PowerShell and JSON. You discovered the history and evolution of PowerShell, the structure and use cases of JSON, and the reasons why using JSON with PowerShell is beneficial. Practical exercises included installing PowerShell, running basic commands, creating and validating JSON objects, and converting between JSON and PowerShell objects.

By mastering the concepts in this chapter, you will be well-prepared to delve deeper into the powerful capabilities of PowerShell and JSON. In the next chapter, we will explore how to get started with PowerShell, including installation, basic commands, and scripting fundamentals.

Chapter 2: Getting Started with PowerShell

Welcome to Chapter 2 of "PowerShell and JSON: From Beginner to Advanced." In this chapter, you will learn how to get started with PowerShell, including installation, basic commands, and introductory scripting. By the end of this chapter, you will be comfortable navigating the PowerShell environment and writing simple scripts.

2.1 Installing PowerShell

Installing PowerShell varies slightly depending on your operating system. PowerShell is available for Windows, macOS, and Linux, making it a versatile tool for cross-platform automation.

Key Points:

- **Windows Installation**: PowerShell comes pre-installed on Windows. You can open it by typing `powershell` in the Start menu or command prompt.
- **macOS Installation**: PowerShell can be installed using Homebrew, a popular package manager for macOS.

- **Linux Installation**: PowerShell can be installed using the package manager for your specific Linux distribution.

Practice:

1. Windows:
    -   Open the Start menu, type `powershell`, and press Enter.
    -   Verify the version by typing `Get-Host` and pressing Enter.
2. macOS:
    -   Open Terminal.
    -   Install Homebrew if not already installed: `/bin/bash -c "$(curl -fsSL https://raw.githubusercontent.com/Homebrew/install/HEAD/install.sh)"`
    -   Install PowerShell: `brew install --cask powershell`
    -   Launch PowerShell: `pwsh`
    -   Verify the version by typing `Get-Host` and pressing Enter.
3. Linux:
    -   Open Terminal.
    -   Install PowerShell using your package manager. For example, on Ubuntu: `sudo apt-get install -y powershell`
    -   Launch PowerShell: `pwsh`
    -   Verify the version by typing `Get-Host` and pressing Enter.

2.2 Basic PowerShell Commands

PowerShell commands, known as cmdlets, are the building blocks of PowerShell. They follow a verb-noun naming convention and are designed to perform specific tasks.

Key Points:

- **Cmdlets**: PowerShell cmdlets are lightweight commands that perform specific functions.
- **Verb-Noun Convention**: Cmdlets are named using a verb-noun convention, such as Get-Process or Set-Location.
- **Common Cmdlets**:
    - `Get-Command`: Lists all available cmdlets.
    - `Get-Help`: Provides help information for cmdlets.
    - `Get-Process`: Displays running processes.
    - `Get-Service`: Displays installed services.

Practice:

1. Explore Cmdlets:
    - List all available cmdlets: `Get-Command`
    - Find information about a specific cmdlet: `Get-Help Get-Process`
2. Basic Commands:
    - Display running processes: `Get-Process`
    - Display installed services: `Get-Service`

- Get the current directory: `Get-Location`
- Change directory: `Set-Location C:\` (replace `C:\` with your desired path)

3. Command Aliases:
   - List all aliases: `Get-Alias`
   - Use an alias: `ls` (alias for `Get-ChildItem`)

2.3 Introduction to PowerShell Scripting

PowerShell scripting allows you to automate tasks by writing scripts, which are sequences of PowerShell commands saved in a `.ps1` file.

Key Points:

- **Script Structure**: PowerShell scripts are plain text files with a `.ps1` extension.
- **Running Scripts**: Scripts can be run by typing their path in the PowerShell console.
- **Basic Constructs**: Scripts can include variables, loops, conditionals, and functions.

Practice:

1. Create and Run a Script:

- Open a text editor and create a file named `HelloWorld.ps1`.
- Add the following content to the file:

```
Write-Output "Hello, World!"
```

- Save the file.
- Open PowerShell and navigate to the directory containing `HelloWorld.ps1`.
- Run the script: `.\HelloWorld.ps1`

2. Using Variables:
   - Create a script named `Variables.ps1` with the following content:

```
$greeting = "Hello"
$name = "Alice"
Write-Output "$greeting, $name!"
```

   - Save and run the script.

3. Conditional Statements:
   - Create a script named `Conditional.ps1` with the following content:

```
$number = 10
if ($number -gt 5) {
   Write-Output "The number is greater than 5."
} else {
   Write-Output "The number is 5 or less."
}
```

   - Save and run the script.

4. Loops:
   - Create a script named `Loop.ps1` with the following content:

```
for ($i = 1; $i -le 5; $i++) {
  Write-Output "Iteration $i"
}
```

- Save and run the script.

5. Functions:

  - Create a script named `Functions.ps1` with the following content:

```
function Greet {
  param ($name)
  Write-Output "Hello, $name!"
}
Greet "Bob"
```

  - Save and run the script.

Quiz

1. How can you install PowerShell on macOS?

   You can install PowerShell on macOS using the following methods:

   - Using Homebrew:

```
brew cask install powershell
```

   - Downloading the .pkg file from the official GitHub repository:

```
https://github.com/PowerShell/PowerShell/releases
Download the latest .pkg file and run it to
install.
```

2. What is the purpose of the Get-Command cmdlet?

The Get-Command cmdlet is used to retrieve information about available commands in PowerShell. It can show you details about cmdlets, functions, aliases, and executables. This is useful for discovering commands, checking syntax, or finding the location of a command.

3. Write a simple PowerShell script that displays your name.

```
Write-Host "Hello, my name is [Your Name]"
```

4. Explain the verb-noun naming convention in PowerShell.

PowerShell uses a verb-noun naming convention for its cmdlets. This convention makes cmdlets more discoverable and self-descriptive:

- The verb describes the action the cmdlet performs (e.g., Get, Set, New, Remove).
- The noun describes the resource on which the cmdlet acts (e.g., Process, Service, Item).

This convention helps users guess command names and understand their purpose more easily.

5. How do you run a PowerShell script?

There are several ways to run a PowerShell script:

- From PowerShell console:

```
.\ScriptName.ps1
```

   - Using the PowerShell executable:

```
powershell -File ScriptName.ps1
```

   - Right-clicking the script in File Explorer and selecting "Run with PowerShell" (on Windows).

   Note: You may need to set the execution policy to allow running scripts:

Remember to navigate to the directory containing your script before running it, or provide the full path to the script file.

In this chapter, you learned how to install PowerShell on different operating systems, execute basic commands, and write simple PowerShell scripts. You explored key PowerShell cmdlets, command aliases, and the basics of scripting, including variables, conditionals, loops, and functions.

By completing this chapter, you have built a solid foundation in PowerShell. In the next chapter, we will delve into understanding JSON syntax and how to work with JSON data in PowerShell.

Chapter 3: Understanding JSON Syntax

Welcome to Chapter 3 of "PowerShell and JSON: From Beginner to Advanced." In this chapter, you will learn about the syntax and structure of JSON (JavaScript Object Notation), a lightweight data interchange format. Understanding JSON syntax is crucial for working with JSON data effectively in PowerShell.

3.1 JSON Data Types

JSON is a text format that is language-independent but uses conventions familiar to programmers of the C family of languages. It is built on two structures: objects and arrays.

Key Points:

- **Strings**: A sequence of characters, enclosed in double quotes.
- **Numbers**: Numeric values, which can be integers or floating-point numbers.
- **Objects**: Collections of key/value pairs, enclosed in curly braces `{ }`.
- **Arrays**: Ordered lists of values, enclosed in square brackets `[ ]`.
- **Booleans**: Logical values, `true` or `false`.
- **Null**: An empty value, represented by `null`.

Practice:

Identify JSON Data Types:

- Review the following JSON snippet and identify the data types:

```
{
  "name": "John Doe",
  "age": 30,
  "is_student": false,
  "courses": ["Math", "Science", "History"],
  "address": {
  "street": "123 Main St",
  "city": "Anytown"
  },
  "graduation_year": null
}
```

- Identify the data types for `name, age, is_student, courses, address,` and `graduation_year`.

3.2 JSON Structure

JSON structure consists of objects and arrays that can be nested within each other to represent complex data hierarchies.

Key Points:

- **Key/Value Pairs**: Objects are made up of key/value pairs, where the key is a string and the value can be any JSON data type.
- **Nested Objects**: Objects can contain other objects as values.

- **Arrays of Values**: Arrays can contain values of any data type, including objects and other arrays.

Practice:

1. **Create a JSON Object:**
   - Write a JSON object that represents a book, including title, author, year, and genres:

```
{
   "title": "PowerShell and JSON",
   "author": "Jane Smith",
   "year": 2024,
   "genres": ["Technology", "Programming"]
}
```

2. **Nested JSON Objects:**
   - Create a JSON object for a company, including name, founded year, and departments (each department should be an object with name and head):

```
{
   "company_name": "Tech Innovations",
   "founded": 2010,
   "departments": [
   {
     "name": "Research and Development",
     "head": "Dr. John Doe"
   },
   {
     "name": "Marketing",
     "head": "Jane Smith"
   }
   ]
```

```
        }
```

3.3 Common JSON Formatting Issues

Properly formatting JSON is crucial to ensure it is valid and can be parsed correctly. Common issues include missing commas, improper use of quotes, and unmatched braces or brackets.

Key Points:

- **Valid JSON**: JSON must be correctly formatted with proper use of commas, quotes, and braces.
- **Common Errors**: Missing commas between key/value pairs, using single quotes instead of double quotes, and mismatched braces or brackets.
- **Troubleshooting**: Use JSON validators and linters to check for syntax errors.

Practice:

1. Identify and Fix Errors:
   - Review the following JSON snippet and correct any formatting errors:

   ```
   {
       'title': 'Learning PowerShell',
   ```

```
    'author': 'Jane Doe'
    'published_year': 2024
    'tags': ['PowerShell', 'Programming',
'Technology']
}
```

- Corrected version:

```
{
    "title": "Learning PowerShell",
    "author": "Jane Doe",
    "published_year": 2024,
    "tags": ["PowerShell", "Programming",
"Technology"]
}
```

2. Validate JSON:

   - Use an online JSON validator (such as **JSONLint**) to validate the following JSON and correct any errors:

```
{
    "product": "Laptop",
    "price": 999.99
    "in_stock": true,
    "specifications": {
    "processor": "Intel i7",
    "memory": "16GB",
    "storage": "512GB SSD"
}
```

3.4 Practice Exercises

Exercise 1: Create a JSON Object

Write a JSON object for a person with name, age, email, and hobbies (an array of strings).

```
{
  "name": "John Doe",
  "age": 30,
  "email": "johndoe@example.com",
  "hobbies": ["reading", "swimming", "photography"]
}
```

Exercise 2: Nested JSON Structure

Create a JSON object representing a school, including name, location, and an array of students (each student should be an object with name, age, and grade).

```
{
  "name": "Springfield High School",
  "location": "Springfield, IL",
  "students": [
    {
      "name": "Lisa Simpson",
      "age": 8,
      "grade": 3
    },
    {
      "name": "Bart Simpson",
      "age": 10,
      "grade": 5
    },
    {
      "name": "Milhouse Van Houten",
```

```
      "age": 10,
      "grade": 5
    }
  ]
}
```

Exercise 3: JSON Array

Write a JSON array of objects, each representing a product with name, price, and availability.

```
[
  {
    "name": "Laptop",
    "price": 999.99,
    "availability": true
  },
  {
    "name": "Smartphone",
    "price": 599.99,
    "availability": false
  },
  {
    "name": "Headphones",
    "price": 149.99,
    "availability": true
  }
]
```

Exercise 4: Validate and Fix JSON

Validate and fix the following JSON:

```
{
  "movie": "Inception",
  "director": "Christopher Nolan"
```

```
  "year": 2010,
  "genres": ["Sci-Fi", "Thriller"],
  "cast": [
    {"actor": "Leonardo DiCaprio", "role": "Cobb"}
    {"actor": "Joseph Gordon-Levitt", "role": "Arthur"}
  ]
}
```

Here's the corrected JSON:

```
{
  "movie": "Inception",
  "director": "Christopher Nolan",
  "year": 2010,
  "genres": ["Sci-Fi", "Thriller"],
  "cast": [
    {"actor": "Leonardo DiCaprio", "role": "Cobb"},
    {"actor": "Joseph Gordon-Levitt", "role": "Arthur"}
  ]
}
```

The fixes were:

1. Added a missing comma after the "director" line
2. Added a missing comma between the cast objects

Exercise 5: JSON Data Types

Create a JSON object that includes all JSON data types (string, number, object, array, boolean, null).

```
{
  "string": "This is a string",
  "number": 42,
  "object": {
    "key": "value"
  },
  "array": [1, 2, 3, 4],
```

```
    "boolean": true,
    "nullValue": null
}
```

This JSON object includes all the main JSON data types: string, number, object, array, boolean, and null.

Quiz

1. What are the six data types in JSON?

    a) String

    b) Number

    c) Boolean

    d) Object

    e) Array

    f) Null

2. How are objects and arrays represented in JSON?

    Objects: Enclosed in curly braces {} with key-value pairs separated by commas.

    Example: {"name": "John", "age": 30}

    Arrays: Enclosed in square brackets [] with values separated by commas.

    Example: ["apple", "banana", "cherry"]

3. What are some common JSON formatting errors?

a) Missing or misplaced commas between elements

b) Using single quotes instead of double quotes for strings

c) Trailing commas (after the last element in an object or array)

d) Unquoted keys in objects

e) Using comments (JSON doesn't support comments)

f) Incorrect nesting of objects and arrays

g) Using undefined as a value (it's not a valid JSON type)

4. Write a JSON object representing a car with make, model, year, and features (array).

```
{
    "make": "Toyota",
    "model": "Camry",
    "year": 2022,
    "features": [
     "Bluetooth",
     "Backup Camera",
     "Lane Departure Warning",
     "Adaptive Cruise Control"
    ]
}
```

This JSON object includes a string for make and model, a number for year, and an array of strings for features.

In this chapter, you learned about the syntax and structure of JSON. You explored JSON data types, how to create and interpret JSON objects and arrays, and how to identify and correct common JSON formatting issues. Practical exercises helped you apply these concepts.

By mastering JSON syntax and structure, you are now ready to start working with JSON data in PowerShell. In the next chapter, we will explore how to parse, create, and manipulate JSON data using PowerShell cmdlets.

Chapter 4: Working with JSON in PowerShell

Welcome to Chapter 4 of "PowerShell and JSON: From Beginner to Advanced." This chapter focuses on how to work with JSON data in PowerShell. You will learn how to parse JSON into PowerShell objects, create JSON from PowerShell objects, and manipulate JSON data. By the end of this chapter, you will be able to handle JSON data efficiently in PowerShell scripts.

4.1 Parsing JSON

Parsing JSON involves converting a JSON string into a PowerShell object. This allows you to interact with the data using PowerShell's object-oriented features.

Key Points:

- **ConvertFrom-Json Cmdlet**: PowerShell cmdlet used to convert a JSON string into a PowerShell object.
- **Handling Nested JSON**: Nested JSON objects and arrays can be accessed using dot notation.

Practice:

1. Parse a Simple JSON String:

   - Open PowerShell and create a JSON string:

   ```
   $jsonString = '{"name": "John Doe", "age": 30,
   "email": "john.doe@example.com"}'
   ```

   - Parse the JSON string:

   ```
   $person = $jsonString | ConvertFrom-Json
   ```

   - Access properties of the parsed object:

   ```
   $person.name
   $person.age
   $person.email
   ```

2. Parse a Nested JSON String:

   - Create a nested JSON string:

   ```
   $jsonString = '{
      "name": "Tech Innovations",
      "founded": 2010,
      "departments": [
          {"name": "Research and Development", "head":
   "Dr. John Doe"},
          {"name": "Marketing", "head": "Jane Smith"}
      ]
   }'
   ```

   - Parse the nested JSON string:

   ```
   $company = $jsonString | ConvertFrom-Json
   ```

- Access nested properties:

```
$company.name
$company.departments[0].name
$company.departments[1].head
```

4.2 Creating JSON

Creating JSON involves converting a PowerShell object into a JSON string. This is useful for generating JSON data for APIs or configuration files.

Key Points:

- **ConvertTo-Json Cmdlet**: PowerShell cmdlet used to convert a Power-Shell object into a JSON string.
- **Formatting Options**: You can control the formatting of the JSON output using parameters like -Depth.

Practice:

1. Create a Simple JSON String:
   - Open PowerShell and create a PowerShell object:

```
$person = @{
  name = "Alice"
  age = 28
  email = "alice@example.com"
```

```
}
```

- Convert the object to JSON:

```
$jsonString = $person | ConvertTo-Json
```

- Output the JSON string:

```
$jsonString
```

2. Create a Nested JSON String:
   - Create a nested PowerShell object:

```
$company = @{
    name = "Tech Innovations"
    founded = 2010
    departments = @(
        @{name = "Research and Development"; head =
"Dr. John Doe"},
        @{name = "Marketing"; head = "Jane Smith"}
    )
}
```

- Convert the object to JSON:

```
$jsonString = $company | ConvertTo-Json -Depth 3
```

- Output the JSON string:

```
$jsonString
```

4.3 Modifying JSON Data

Modifying JSON data involves accessing and updating properties of a parsed JSON object. You can add, modify, or remove properties as needed.

Key Points:

- **Accessing Properties**: Use dot notation to access properties of a JSON object.
- **Updating Properties**: Assign new values to properties to update them.
- **Adding Properties**: Add new key/value pairs to the object.
- **Removing Properties**: Use the Remove-Property method to remove properties.

Practice:

1. Modify Properties of a JSON Object:
   - Parse a JSON string:

     ```
     $jsonString = '{"name": "Bob", "age": 35, "email":
     "bob@example.com"}'
     $person = $jsonString | ConvertFrom-Json
     ```

   - Modify a property:

     ```
     $person.age = 36
     ```

   - Add a new property:

```
$person.phone = "123-456-7890"
```

- Remove a property:

```
$person.PSObject.Properties.Remove("email")
```

- Convert back to JSON:

```
$jsonString = $person | ConvertTo-Json
$jsonString
```

2. Modify Nested JSON Data:
   - Parse a nested JSON string:

```
$jsonString = '{
    "name": "Tech Innovations",
    "founded": 2010,
    "departments": [
        {"name": "Research and Development", "head":
"Dr. John Doe"},
        {"name": "Marketing", "head": "Jane Smith"}
    ]
}'
$company = $jsonString | ConvertFrom-Json
```

- Update a nested property:

```
$company.departments[0].head = "Dr. Alice Johnson"
```

- Add a new department:

```
$company.departments += @{name = "Human
Resources"; head = "Michael Brown"}
```

- Convert back to JSON:

```
$jsonString = $company | ConvertTo-Json -Depth 3
$jsonString
```

4.4 Practice Exercises

Exercise 1: Parse a JSON Array

Parse a JSON array string and access the elements:

```
$jsonArray = '[{"product": "Laptop", "price": 999.99},
{"product": "Tablet", "price": 499.99}]'
$products = $jsonArray | ConvertFrom-Json
$products[0].product
$products[1].price
```

Exercise 2: Create a JSON Array

Create a PowerShell array of objects and convert it to JSON:

```
$products = @(
    @{product = "Laptop"; price = 999.99},
    @{product = "Tablet"; price = 499.99}
)
$jsonArray = $products | ConvertTo-Json
$jsonArray
```

Exercise 3: Modify a JSON Array

Parse a JSON array, modify an element, and convert it back to JSON:

```
$jsonArray = '[{"product": "Laptop", "price": 999.99},
{"product": "Tablet", "price": 499.99}]'
$products = $jsonArray | ConvertFrom-Json
$products[1].price = 450.00
$jsonArray = $products | ConvertTo-Json
$jsonArray
```

Exercise 4: Add Elements to a JSON Array

Parse a JSON array, add a new element, and convert it back to JSON:

```
$jsonArray = '[{"product": "Laptop", "price": 999.99},
{"product": "Tablet", "price": 499.99}]'
$products = $jsonArray | ConvertFrom-Json
$products += @{product = "Smartphone"; price = 299.99}
$jsonArray = $products | ConvertTo-Json
$jsonArray
```

Exercise 5: Remove Elements from a JSON Array

Parse a JSON array, remove an element, and convert it back to JSON:

```
$jsonArray = '[{"product": "Laptop", "price": 999.99},
{"product": "Tablet", "price": 499.99}]'
$products = $jsonArray | ConvertFrom-Json
$products = $products | Where-Object { $_.product -ne "Tablet" }
$jsonArray = $products | ConvertTo-Json
$jsonArray
```

Quiz

1. What cmdlet is used to convert a JSON string to a PowerShell object?

   ```
   ConvertFrom-Json
   ```

2. How do you convert a PowerShell object to a JSON string?

   ```
   ConvertTo-Json
   ```

3. Write a PowerShell script to parse a JSON string representing a book (with title, author, and year), modify the year, and convert it back to JSON.

   ```
   # JSON string representing a book
   $jsonString = '{"title": "The Great Gatsby", "author":
   "F. Scott Fitzgerald", "year": 1925}'

   # Convert JSON to PowerShell object
   $book = $jsonString | ConvertFrom-Json

   # Modify the year
   $book.year = 2023

   # Convert back to JSON
   $updatedJsonString = $book | ConvertTo-Json

   # Output the result
   Write-Output $updatedJsonString
   ```

4. How can you add a new property to a parsed JSON object in Power-Shell?

   ```
   $jsonObject = '{"name": "John", "age": 30}' |
   ConvertFrom-Json
   $jsonObject | Add-Member -MemberType NoteProperty -Name
   "city" -Value "New York"
   ```

5. Write a PowerShell script to parse a JSON array of products, add a new product, and convert it back to JSON.

```powershell
# JSON string representing an array of products
$jsonString = '[
    {"name": "Apple", "price": 0.5},
    {"name": "Banana", "price": 0.3},
    {"name": "Orange", "price": 0.6}
]'

# Convert JSON to PowerShell object
$products = $jsonString | ConvertFrom-Json

# Create a new product
$newProduct = @{
    name = "Grape"
    price = 0.8
}

# Add the new product to the array
$products += $newProduct

# Convert back to JSON
$updatedJsonString = $products | ConvertTo-Json

# Output the result
Write-Output $updatedJsonString
```

These examples demonstrate how to work with JSON in PowerShell, including parsing, modifying, and converting back to JSON. The ConvertFrom-Json and ConvertTo-Json cmdlets are key to these operations, allowing seamless conversion between JSON strings and PowerShell objects.

In this chapter, you learned how to work with JSON data in PowerShell. You explored how to parse JSON strings into PowerShell objects, create JSON from PowerShell objects, and modify JSON data. Practical exercises helped reinforce these concepts.

By mastering these techniques, you are now well-equipped to handle JSON data in PowerShell scripts. In the next chapter, we will delve into advanced JSON manipulation techniques for handling complex data structures.

Chapter 5: Advanced JSON Manipulation

Welcome to Chapter 5 of "PowerShell and JSON: From Beginner to Advanced." This chapter will focus on advanced techniques for manipulating JSON data in PowerShell. You will learn how to work with complex JSON structures, filter JSON data, and merge or combine JSON objects and arrays. These skills will enable you to handle sophisticated JSON data manipulation tasks effectively.

5.1 Working with Complex JSON Structures

Complex JSON structures often involve deeply nested objects and arrays. Understanding how to navigate and manipulate these structures is crucial for advanced JSON handling in PowerShell.

Key Points:

- **Nested JSON Objects**: JSON objects can contain other objects as values, creating a hierarchical structure.
- **JSON Arrays**: Arrays can contain objects, which may themselves contain arrays or other objects.

- **Accessing Nested Data**: Use dot notation and array indexing to access nested properties and elements.

Practice:

1. Parse a Complex JSON String:
   - Open PowerShell and create a complex JSON string:

```
$jsonString = '{
   "company": "Tech Innovations",
   "employees": [
       {
           "name": "Alice",
           "position": "Developer",
           "skills": ["C#", "PowerShell",
"JavaScript"]
       },
       {
           "name": "Bob",
           "position": "Manager",
           "skills": ["Management",
"Communication"]
       }
   ]
}'
```

   - Parse the JSON string:

```
$data = $jsonString | ConvertFrom-Json
```

   - Access nested properties:

```
$data.company
$data.employees[0].name
$data.employees[1].skills[1]
```

2. Modify Nested JSON Data:

- Change a nested property:

```
$data.employees[0].position = "Senior Developer"
```

- Add a new skill to an employee:

```
$data.employees[1].skills += "Leadership"
```

- Convert back to JSON:

```
$jsonString = $data | ConvertTo-Json -Depth 3
$jsonString
```

5.2 Filtering JSON Data

Filtering JSON data involves extracting specific elements or objects from a JSON structure based on certain criteria. This is particularly useful for processing large JSON datasets.

Key Points:

- **Where-Object Cmdlet**: Use `Where-Object` to filter PowerShell objects based on conditions.
- **Conditional Logic**: Apply conditions to filter nested JSON data.

Practice:

1. Filter JSON Array Elements:
   - Parse a JSON array:

   ```
   $jsonArray = '[{"name": "Alice", "age": 28},
   {"name": "Bob", "age": 35}, {"name": "Charlie",
   "age": 30}]'
   $people = $jsonArray | ConvertFrom-Json
   ```

   - Filter elements where age is greater than 30:

   ```
   $olderThan30 = $people | Where-Object { $_.age -gt
   30 }
   $olderThan30
   ```

2. Filter Nested JSON Data:
   - Parse a nested JSON string:

   ```
   $jsonString = '{
      "company": "Tech Innovations",
      "employees": [
          {"name": "Alice", "age": 28, "position":
   "Developer"},
          {"name": "Bob", "age": 35, "position":
   "Manager"},
          {"name": "Charlie", "age": 30, "position":
   "Analyst"}
      ]
   }'
   $data = $jsonString | ConvertFrom-Json
   ```

   - Filter employees based on position:

   ```
   $developers = $data.employees | Where-Object
   { $_.position -eq "Developer" }
   ```

5.3 Merging and Combining JSON Data

Merging and combining JSON data involves integrating multiple JSON objects or arrays into a single structure. This is useful for consolidating data from various sources.

Key Points:

- **Combining JSON Arrays**: Use the addition operator (+=) to merge arrays.
- **Merging JSON Objects**: Combine properties of multiple objects into a single object.

Practice:

1. Combine JSON Arrays:
   - Parse two JSON arrays:

```
$jsonArray1 = '[{"name": "Alice", "age": 28},
{"name": "Bob", "age": 35}]'
$jsonArray2 = '[{"name": "Charlie", "age": 30},
{"name": "David", "age": 40}]'
$array1 = $jsonArray1 | ConvertFrom-Json
$array2 = $jsonArray2 | ConvertFrom-Json
```

- Combine the arrays:

```
$combinedArray = $array1 + $array2
$combinedArray
```

2. Merge JSON Objects:

- Create two PowerShell objects:

```
$object1 = @{
   name = "Alice"
   age = 28
}
$object2 = @{
   position = "Developer"
   skills = @("C#", "PowerShell")
}
```

- Merge the objects:

```
$mergedObject = [PSCustomObject]@{ name =
$object1.name; age = $object1.age; position =
$object2.position; skills = $object2.skills }
$mergedObject
```

- Convert the merged object to JSON:

```
$jsonString = $mergedObject | ConvertTo-Json
$jsonString
```

5.4 Practice Exercises

Exercise 1: Access Deeply Nested JSON Data

Parse a deeply nested JSON string and access specific elements:

```
$jsonString = '{
    "university": "Tech University",
    "departments": [
        {
            "name": "Computer Science",
            "courses": [
                {"name": "Algorithms", "code": "CS101"},
                {"name": "Data Structures", "code": "CS102"}
            ]
        },
        {
            "name": "Mathematics",
            "courses": [
                {"name": "Calculus", "code": "MATH101"},
                {"name": "Linear Algebra", "code": "MATH102"}
            ]
        }
    ]
}'
$data = $jsonString | ConvertFrom-Json
$data.departments[0].courses[1].name
```

Exercise 2: Filter JSON Array Based on Multiple Conditions

Parse a JSON array and filter elements based on multiple conditions:

```
$jsonArray = '[{"name": "Alice", "age": 28, "position":
"Developer"}, {"name": "Bob", "age": 35, "position": "Manager"},
{"name": "Charlie", "age": 30, "position": "Analyst"}]'
$employees = $jsonArray | ConvertFrom-Json
$filteredEmployees = $employees | Where-Object { $_.age -gt 30
-and $_.position -eq "Manager" }
$filteredEmployees
```

Exercise 3: Merge Multiple JSON Objects

Parse multiple JSON objects and merge them into a single object:

```
$jsonString1 = '{"name": "Alice", "age": 28}'
$jsonString2 = '{"position": "Developer", "skills": ["C#",
"PowerShell"]}'
$object1 = $jsonString1 | ConvertFrom-Json
$object2 = $jsonString2 | ConvertFrom-Json
$mergedObject = [PSCustomObject]@{ name = $object1.name; age =
$object1.age; position = $object2.position; skills =
$object2.skills }
$mergedObject
```

Exercise 4: Combine and Filter JSON Arrays

Parse and combine two JSON arrays, then filter the combined array:

```
$jsonArray1 = '[{"name": "Alice", "age": 28}, {"name": "Bob",
"age": 35}]'
$jsonArray2 = '[{"name": "Charlie", "age": 30}, {"name": "David",
"age": 40}]'
$array1 = $jsonArray1 | ConvertFrom-Json
$array2 = $jsonArray2 | ConvertFrom-Json
$combinedArray = $array1 + $array2
$filteredArray = $combinedArray | Where-Object { $_.age -gt 30 }
$filteredArray
```

Exercise 5: Modify and Serialize Complex JSON Data

Parse a complex JSON string, modify its content, and convert it back to JSON:

```
$jsonString = '{
    "project": "Tech Upgrade",
    "team": [
        {"name": "Alice", "role": "Developer"},
        {"name": "Bob", "role": "Manager"}
    ],
    "deadline": "2024-12-31"
}'
$project = $jsonString | ConvertFrom-Json
$project.team[1].role = "Senior Manager"
$project.team += @{name = "Charlie"; role = "Tester"}
$jsonString = $project | ConvertTo-Json -Depth 3
$jsonString
```

Quiz

1. How do you access a nested property in a JSON object in PowerShell?
   You can access nested properties using dot notation or square brackets.

   ```
   $json = '{"user": {"name": "John", "age": 30}}'
       $obj = $json | ConvertFrom-Json
       $name = $obj.user.name
       # or
       $name = $obj.user['name']
   ```

2. What cmdlet is used to filter JSON data based on conditions?

   The `Where-Object` cmdlet is commonly used to filter JSON data after converting it to PowerShell objects.

3. Write a PowerShell script to parse a JSON array of employees, filter those who are developers, and convert the filtered data back to JSON.

```
$jsonData = '[
    {"name": "John", "role": "developer"},
    {"name": "Alice", "role": "manager"},
    {"name": "Bob", "role": "developer"}
    ]'

    $employees = $jsonData | ConvertFrom-Json
    $developers = $employees | Where-Object { $_.role -eq
"developer" }
    $filteredJson = $developers | ConvertTo-Json

    Write-Output $filteredJson
```

4. How can you combine two JSON arrays in PowerShell?

   You can use the + operator to combine arrays after converting them from JSON:

```
$json1 = '[{"id": 1}, {"id": 2}]'
    $json2 = '[{"id": 3}, {"id": 4}]'

    $array1 = $json1 | ConvertFrom-Json
    $array2 = $json2 | ConvertFrom-Json

    $combinedArray = $array1 + $array2
    $combinedJson = $combinedArray | ConvertTo-Json

    Write-Output $combinedJson
```

5. Write a PowerShell script to merge two JSON objects with different properties and convert the merged object to JSON.

```
$json1 = '{"name": "John", "age": 30}'
```

```
$json2 = '{"city": "New York", "job": "developer"}'

$obj1 = $json1 | ConvertFrom-Json
$obj2 = $json2 | ConvertFrom-Json

$mergedObj = @{}
$obj1.PSObject.Properties | ForEach-Object
{ $mergedObj[$_.Name] = $_.Value }
$obj2.PSObject.Properties | ForEach-Object
{ $mergedObj[$_.Name] = $_.Value }

$mergedJson = $mergedObj | ConvertTo-Json

Write-Output $mergedJson
```

This script creates a new hashtable $mergedObj and adds properties from both objects to it. Then it converts the merged object back to JSON.

In this chapter, you learned advanced techniques for manipulating JSON data in PowerShell. You explored how to work with complex JSON structures, filter JSON data based on specific criteria, and merge or combine JSON objects and arrays. Practical exercises helped you apply these concepts to real-world scenarios.

By mastering these advanced techniques, you are now well-equipped to handle complex JSON manipulation tasks in PowerShell. In the next chapter, we will explore integrating JSON with external services and automating API interactions.

Chapter 6: Integrating JSON with External Services

Welcome to Chapter 6 of "PowerShell and JSON: From Beginner to Advanced." In this chapter, you will learn how to integrate JSON with external services using PowerShell. This includes consuming web APIs, automating API interactions, and storing and retrieving JSON data. By the end of this chapter, you will be able to interact with various external services and APIs using JSON and PowerShell.

6.1 Consuming Web APIs

Web APIs (Application Programming Interfaces) allow applications to communicate with each other over the internet. JSON is commonly used for the data exchanged in these interactions. PowerShell can be used to send HTTP requests to web APIs and handle their JSON responses.

Key Points:

- **HTTP Methods**: Common methods include GET (retrieve data), POST (send data), PUT (update data), and DELETE (remove data).
- **Invoke-RestMethod Cmdlet**: PowerShell cmdlet used to send HTTP requests to web APIs and process JSON responses.

Practice:

1. Send a GET Request:

   - Use `Invoke-RestMethod` to send a GET request to a public API:

   ```
   $url = "https://jsonplaceholder.typicode.com/
   posts/1"
   $response = Invoke-RestMethod -Uri $url -Method
   Get
   $response
   ```

2. Send a POST Request:

   - Use `Invoke-RestMethod` to send a POST request with JSON data:

   ```
   $url = "https://jsonplaceholder.typicode.com/
   posts"
   $body = @{
       title = "foo"
       body = "bar"
       userId = 1
   } | ConvertTo-Json
   $response = Invoke-RestMethod -Uri $url -Method
   Post -Body $body -ContentType "application/json"
   $response
   ```

6.2 Automating API Interactions

Automating API interactions involves creating reusable PowerShell scripts or functions to handle repetitive tasks such as fetching data, updating records, or deleting entries. This can significantly streamline workflows and improve efficiency.

Key Points:

- **Reusable Functions**: Create PowerShell functions to encapsulate API interactions.
- **Error Handling**: Implement error handling to manage failed requests or invalid responses.

Practice:

1. Create a Function to Fetch Data:
   - Define a PowerShell function to fetch data from an API:

   ```
   function Get-Post {
     param (
         [int]$postId
     )
     $url = "https://jsonplaceholder.typicode.com/
   posts/$postId"
     $response = Invoke-RestMethod -Uri $url -Method
   Get
     return $response
   }
   ```

   - Call the function:

   ```
   $post = Get-Post -postId 1
   $post
   ```

2. Create a Function to Send Data:
   - Define a PowerShell function to send data to an API:

   ```
   function New-Post {
     param (
   ```

```
        [string]$title,
        [string]$body,
        [int]$userId
    )
    $url = "https://jsonplaceholder.typicode.com/
posts"
    $postBody = @{
        title = $title
        body = $body
        userId = $userId
    } | ConvertTo-Json
    $response = Invoke-RestMethod -Uri $url -Method
Post -Body $postBody -ContentType "application/
json"
    return $response
}
```

- Call the function:

```
$newPost = New-Post -title "My New Post" -body
"This is the content of my new post." -userId 1
$newPost
```

6.3 Storing and Retrieving JSON Data

Storing and retrieving JSON data involves saving JSON responses to files and reading JSON data from files. This is useful for persisting data and processing it later.

Key Points:

- **Saving JSON to Files**: Use `Out-File` or `Set-Content` to save JSON data to a file.
- **Reading JSON from Files**: Use `Get-Content` to read JSON data from a file and convert it back to a PowerShell object.

Practice:

1. Save JSON Data to a File:
   - Fetch data from an API and save it to a file:

   ```
   $url = "https://jsonplaceholder.typicode.com/
   posts/1"
   $response = Invoke-RestMethod -Uri $url -Method
   Get
   $jsonString = $response | ConvertTo-Json
   $jsonString | Out-File -FilePath "post.json"
   ```

2. Read JSON Data from a File:
   - Read JSON data from a file and convert it back to a PowerShell object:

   ```
   $jsonString = Get-Content -Path "post.json" -Raw
   $post = $jsonString | ConvertFrom-Json
   $post
   ```

6.4 Practice Exercises

Exercise 1: Fetch User Data from an API

Use `Invoke-RestMethod` to fetch data about a user from a public API and display their name and email:

```
$url = "https://jsonplaceholder.typicode.com/users/1"
$user = Invoke-RestMethod -Uri $url -Method Get
$user.name
$user.email
```

Exercise 2: Create a Function to Update Data

Define a PowerShell function to update a post using the PUT method:

```
function Update-Post {
    param (
        [int]$postId,
        [string]$title,
        [string]$body
    )
    $url = "https://jsonplaceholder.typicode.com/posts/$postId"
    $postBody = @{
        id = $postId
        title = $title
        body = $body
        userId = 1
    } | ConvertTo-Json
    $response = Invoke-RestMethod -Uri $url -Method Put -Body
$postBody -ContentType "application/json"
    return $response
}
```

Call the function to update a post:

```
$updatedPost = Update-Post -postId 1 -title "Updated Title" -body
"Updated content."
$updatedPost
```

Exercise 3: Store and Retrieve Multiple JSON Objects

Fetch a list of posts from an API and save them to a file:

```
$url = "https://jsonplaceholder.typicode.com/posts"
$posts = Invoke-RestMethod -Uri $url -Method Get
$jsonString = $posts | ConvertTo-Json
$jsonString | Out-File -FilePath "posts.json"
```

Read the list of posts from the file and filter posts by a specific userId:

```
$jsonString = Get-Content -Path "posts.json" -Raw
$posts = $jsonString | ConvertFrom-Json
$userPosts = $posts | Where-Object { $_.userId -eq 1 }
$userPosts
```

Exercise 4: Automate API Interaction to Delete Data

Define a PowerShell function to delete a post using the DELETE method:

```
function Remove-Post {
    param (
        [int]$postId
    )
    $url = "https://jsonplaceholder.typicode.com/posts/$postId"
    Invoke-RestMethod -Uri $url -Method Delete
```

```
        return "Post $postId deleted."
}
```

Call the function to delete a post:

```
$result = Remove-Post -postId 1
$result
```

Exercise 5: Handle API Response Errors

Define a PowerShell function to fetch data from an API with error handling:

```
function Get-Data {
    param (
        [string]$url
    )
    try {
        $response = Invoke-RestMethod -Uri $url -Method Get
        return $response
    } catch {
        Write-Error "Failed to fetch data from $url. $_"
    }
}
```

Call the function with a valid URL and an invalid URL to test error handling:

```
$validUrl = "https://jsonplaceholder.typicode.com/posts/1"
$invalidUrl = "https://invalidurl.com/posts"
$data = Get-Data -url $validUrl
$data
$data = Get-Data -url $invalidUrl
$data
```

Quiz

1. What cmdlet is used to send HTTP requests to web APIs in PowerShell?

```
Invoke-RestMethod
```

You can also use `Invoke-WebRequest`, but `Invoke-RestMethod` is generally preferred for API interactions as it automatically parses the response into PowerShell objects.

2. How do you send a POST request with JSON data using PowerShell?

```
$body = @{
      key1 = "value1"
      key2 = "value2"
   } | ConvertTo-Json

   $response = Invoke-RestMethod -Uri "https://
api.example.com/endpoint" -Method Post -Body $body
-ContentType "application/json"
```

3. Write a PowerShell function to fetch data from an API and handle errors.

```
function Get-APIData {
      param (
            [string]$Url
      )

      try {
            $response = Invoke-RestMethod -Uri $Url
-ErrorAction Stop
            return $response
      }
      catch [System.Net.WebException] {
            Write-Error "HTTP request failed. Status code:
$($_.Exception.Response.StatusCode.value__)"
      }
      catch {
            Write-Error "An error occurred: $_"
      }
```

```
    }

    # Usage
    $data = Get-APIData -Url "https://api.example.com/
data"
    if ($data) {
       # Process the data
    }
```

4. How can you save JSON data to a file in PowerShell?

```
    $data = @{
        name = "John Doe"
        age = 30
    }

    $data | ConvertTo-Json | Out-File -FilePath
"data.json"
```

5. Write a PowerShell script to read JSON data from a file and filter the data based on a specific criterion.

```
# Read JSON data from file
    $jsonData = Get-Content -Path "data.json" |
ConvertFrom-Json

    # Filter data based on a criterion (e.g., age greater
than 25)
    $filteredData = $jsonData | Where-Object { $_.age -gt
25 }

    # Display filtered data
    $filteredData | Format-Table

    # Optionally, save filtered data to a new JSON file
    $filteredData | ConvertTo-Json | Out-File -FilePath
"filtered_data.json"
```

This script assumes that the JSON file contains an array of objects. If it's a single object or has a different structure, you might need to adjust the filtering logic accordingly.

These examples cover the basics of working with APIs and JSON data in PowerShell. Remember to replace placeholder URLs, file paths, and data structures with your actual values when using these scripts.

In this chapter, you learned how to integrate JSON with external services using PowerShell. You explored how to consume web APIs, automate API interactions, and store and retrieve JSON data. Practical exercises helped you apply these concepts to real-world scenarios.

By mastering these integration techniques, you are now well-equipped to handle API interactions and integrate JSON with external services using PowerShell. In the next chapter, we will delve into advanced PowerShell scripting with JSON, including dynamic JSON processing and performance optimization.

Chapter 7: Advanced Power-Shell Scripting with JSON

Welcome to Chapter 7 of "PowerShell and JSON: From Beginner to Advanced." In this chapter, you will learn advanced PowerShell scripting techniques for working with JSON data. This includes creating JSON schemas, dynamic JSON processing, and performance optimization. By the end of this chapter, you will be able to handle complex JSON data and optimize your scripts for better performance.

7.1 Creating JSON Schemas

A JSON Schema is a vocabulary that allows you to annotate and validate JSON documents. It defines the structure and constraints of JSON data, ensuring the data adheres to a specific format.

Key Points:

- **JSON Schema Structure**: Consists of properties, types, and constraints to define the expected structure of JSON data.
- **Validation**: Ensures JSON data matches the defined schema, which is crucial for data integrity and consistency.

Practice:

1. Define a Simple JSON Schema:

   - Create a JSON schema for a user object:

```json
{
    "$schema": "http://json-schema.org/draft-07/
schema#",
    "title": "User",
    "type": "object",
    "properties": {
        "name": {
            "type": "string"
        },
        "age": {
            "type": "integer",
            "minimum": 0
        },
        "email": {
            "type": "string",
            "format": "email"
        }
    },
    "required": ["name", "email"]
}
```

2. Validate JSON Data Against Schema:

   - Use PowerShell with a JSON schema validation library (like New-tonsoft.Json.Schema):

```powershell
Install-Package Newtonsoft.Json.Schema

$schema = '{
    "$schema": "http://json-schema.org/draft-07/
schema#",
    "title": "User",
    "type": "object",
    "properties": {
```

```powershell
      "name": { "type": "string" },
      "age": { "type": "integer", "minimum": 0 },
      "email": { "type": "string", "format":
"email" }
  },
  "required": ["name", "email"]
}'

$json = '{"name": "Alice", "age": 28, "email":
"alice@example.com"}'
$JSchema =
[Newtonsoft.Json.Schema.JSchema]::Parse($schema)
$JObject =
[Newtonsoft.Json.Linq.JObject]::Parse($json)
$isValid = $JObject.IsValid($JSchema)
$isValid
```

7.2 Dynamic JSON Processing

Dynamic JSON processing involves working with JSON data that may have an unknown structure at runtime. This requires the use of dynamic objects and reflection to handle such data flexibly.

Key Points:

- **Dynamic Objects**: Use PowerShell's dynamic object features to work with JSON data of unknown structure.
- **Reflection**: Inspect and manipulate JSON data at runtime without knowing its structure in advance.

Practice:

1. Parse and Access Dynamic JSON Data:

   - Parse JSON data with an unknown structure:

     ```
     $jsonString = '{
       "id": 1,
       "details": {
           "name": "Alice",
           "roles": ["Admin", "User"]
       },
       "settings": {
           "theme": "dark",
           "notifications": true
       }
     }'
     $data = $jsonString | ConvertFrom-Json
     ```

   - Access properties dynamically:

     ```
     foreach ($property in $data.PSObject.Properties) {
       Write-Output "Property Name: $($property.Name)"
       Write-Output "Property Value: $
     ($property.Value)"
     }
     ```

2. Modify Dynamic JSON Data:

   - Add a new property dynamically:

     ```
     $data.PSObject.Properties.Add([PSNoteProperty]::ne
     w("newProperty", "newValue"))
     ```

   - Remove a property dynamically:

     ```
     $data.PSObject.Properties.Remove("id")
     ```

- Convert back to JSON:

```
$jsonString = $data | ConvertTo-Json -Depth 3
$jsonString
```

7.3 Performance Optimization

Optimizing the performance of PowerShell scripts that handle JSON data involves minimizing memory usage and execution time. This is particularly important when dealing with large JSON datasets.

Key Points:

- **Efficient Parsing and Generation**: Use efficient methods for parsing and generating JSON to reduce overhead.
- **Memory Management**: Manage memory usage by properly handling large datasets and releasing resources when they are no longer needed.

Practice:

1. Efficient Parsing of Large JSON Data:
   - Use streaming techniques to parse large JSON files:

```
$filePath = "largeData.json"
$stream = [System.IO.StreamReader]::new($filePath)
while ($line = $stream.ReadLine()) {
```

```
    $jsonObject = $line | ConvertFrom-Json
    # Process each JSON object here
}
$stream.Close()
```

2. Optimize JSON Generation:

- Use `ConvertTo-Json` with the `-Compress` parameter for faster generation:

```
$data = @{
    name = "Alice"
    age = 28
    email = "alice@example.com"
}
$jsonString = $data | ConvertTo-Json -Compress
$jsonString
```

3. Memory Management:

- Release resources after processing large JSON datasets:

```
$data = $null
[GC]::Collect()
```

7.4 Practice Exercises

Exercise 1: Validate JSON Data with Schema

Create a JSON schema for a product object (`name`, `price`, `in_stock`) and validate JSON data against it:

```
$schema = '{
    "$schema": "http://json-schema.org/draft-07/schema#",
    "title": "Product",
    "type": "object",
    "properties": {
        "name": { "type": "string" },
        "price": { "type": "number" },
        "in_stock": { "type": "boolean" }
    },
    "required": ["name", "price"]
}'

$json = '{"name": "Laptop", "price": 999.99, "in_stock": true}'
$JSchema = [Newtonsoft.Json.Schema.JSchema]::Parse($schema)
$JObject = [Newtonsoft.Json.Linq.JObject]::Parse($json)
$isValid = $JObject.IsValid($JSchema)
$isValid
```

Exercise 2: Access and Modify Dynamic JSON Data

Parse a dynamic JSON string, add a new property, and remove an existing property:

```
$jsonString = '{
    "username": "user1",
    "attributes": {
        "height": 170,
        "weight": 70
    },
    "preferences": {
        "language": "English",
        "timezone": "UTC"
    }
}'
$data = $jsonString | ConvertFrom-Json
$data.PSObject.Properties.Add([PSNoteProperty]::new("status",
"active"))
$data.PSObject.Properties.Remove("preferences")
```

```powershell
$jsonString = $data | ConvertTo-Json -Depth 3
$jsonString
```

Exercise 3: Efficiently Parse a Large JSON File

Use streaming to efficiently parse a large JSON file and process each object:

```powershell
$filePath = "largeData.json"
$stream = [System.IO.StreamReader]::new($filePath)
while ($line = $stream.ReadLine()) {
    $jsonObject = $line | ConvertFrom-Json
    # Process each JSON object here
}
$stream.Close()
```

Exercise 4: Optimize JSON Generation

Generate a compressed JSON string from a PowerShell object:

```powershell
$data = @{
    username = "user1"
    age = 30
    email = "user1@example.com"
    roles = @("admin", "user")
}
$jsonString = $data | ConvertTo-Json -Compress
$jsonString
```

Exercise 5: Manage Memory Efficiently

Process a large JSON dataset and release memory after processing:

```
$jsonString = Get-Content -Path "largeData.json" -Raw
$data = $jsonString | ConvertFrom-Json
# Process the data here
$data = $null
[GC]::Collect()
```

Quiz

1. What is a JSON Schema, and why is it used?

   A JSON Schema is a declarative format for describing the structure, content, and constraints of JSON data. It's used for:

   - Validating JSON data

   - Documenting JSON APIs

   - Generating code, forms, or databases based on the schema

   - Enabling auto-completion and validation in IDEs

   JSON Schema helps ensure data quality, provides clear documentation, and facilitates interoperability between systems.

2. How can you dynamically access properties of a JSON object in Power-Shell?

   You can use dot notation or square bracket notation to access JSON properties dynamically:

   ```
   $json = '{"name": "John", "age": 30}'
   $obj = $json | ConvertFrom-Json

   # Dot notation
   $obj.name

   # Square bracket notation
   $obj.'name'
   $obj['name']
   ```

```
# For dynamic property names
$prop = 'name'
$obj.$prop
```

3. Write a PowerShell function to validate JSON data against a given schema.

   Here's a basic function that uses the `Newtonsoft.Json.Schema` NuGet package:

```
function Test-JsonSchema {
    param (
        [string]$JsonData,
        [string]$SchemaJson
    )

    # Ensure Newtonsoft.Json.Schema is installed
    if (-not (Get-Package -Name Newtonsoft.Json.Schema
-ErrorAction SilentlyContinue)) {
        Install-Package Newtonsoft.Json.Schema -Scope
CurrentUser -Force
    }

    Add-Type -Path (Get-Package
Newtonsoft.Json.Schema).Source

    $schema =
[Newtonsoft.Json.Schema.JSchema]::Parse($SchemaJson)
    $jsonObject =
[Newtonsoft.Json.Linq.JObject]::Parse($JsonData)

    $isValid = $jsonObject.IsValid($schema, [ref]$null)

    return $isValid
}

# Usage
$schema = '{"type": "object", "properties": {"name":
{"type": "string"}, "age": {"type": "integer"}}}'
$json = '{"name": "John", "age": 30}'
```

```
Test-JsonSchema -JsonData $json -SchemaJson $schema
```

4. How can you efficiently parse large JSON files in PowerShell?

For large JSON files, use streaming techniques:

```
$jsonStream = [System.IO.File]::OpenText("large-
file.json")
try {
    $jsonReader = New-Object -TypeName
Newtonsoft.Json.JsonTextReader -ArgumentList $jsonStream
    $serializer = New-Object -TypeName
Newtonsoft.Json.JsonSerializer

    while ($jsonReader.Read()) {
        if ($jsonReader.TokenType -eq 'StartObject') {
            $object =
$serializer.Deserialize($jsonReader)
            # Process $object here
        }
    }
}
finally {
    $jsonStream.Close()
}
```

Another approach for handling large JSON files is to use the -Read-Count parameter with Get-Content and process the file in chunks:

```
$chunkSize = 1000
Get-Content "large-file.json" -ReadCount $chunkSize |
ForEach-Object {
    $chunk = $_ -join ""
    try {
        $jsonObject = $chunk | ConvertFrom-Json
        # Process $jsonObject here
    }
    catch {
        Write-Warning "Error processing chunk: $_"
    }
}
```

This method is useful when the JSON file contains an array of objects, and you can process each object independently.

5. Write a PowerShell script to generate a compressed JSON string from a complex object.

```
function ConvertTo-CompressedJson {
    param (
        [Parameter(Mandatory=$true,
ValueFromPipeline=$true)]
        [object]$InputObject,

        [switch]$IncludeNulls,

        [switch]$IncludeDefaults
    )

    begin {
        Add-Type -AssemblyName System.Web.Extensions
        $jsSerializer = New-Object
System.Web.Script.Serialization.JavaScriptSerializer

        # Increase MaxJsonLength if needed
        $jsSerializer.MaxJsonLength = [int]::MaxValue
    }

    process {
        $jsonSettings = @{
            NullValueHandling = if ($IncludeNulls)
{ 'Include' } else { 'Ignore' }
            DefaultValueHandling = if ($IncludeDefaults)
{ 'Include' } else { 'Ignore' }
        }

        $compressedJson =
$jsSerializer.Serialize($InputObject)

        # Further compression by removing unnecessary
whitespace
        $compressedJson = $compressedJson -replace '"\s*:
\s*"', '":"' -replace '"\s*,\s*"', '","'
```

```powershell
        return $compressedJson
    }
}

# Usage example with a more complex object
$complexObject = @{
    person = @{
        name = "John Doe"
        age = 30
        address = @{
            street = "123 Main St"
            city = "Anytown"
            country = "USA"
        }
    }
    orders = @(
        @{
            id = 1
            items = @("book", "pen")
            total = 25.50
        },
        @{
            id = 2
            items = @("laptop", "mouse")
            total = 1200.00
        }
    )
    preferences = @{
        newsletter = $true
        theme = "dark"
    }
    lastLogin = Get-Date
}

$compressedJson = $complexObject | ConvertTo-
CompressedJson
Write-Output $compressedJson
```

In this chapter, you learned advanced PowerShell scripting techniques for working with JSON data. You explored how to create and validate JSON schemas, process dynamic JSON data, and optimize your scripts for better performance. Practical exercises helped you apply these concepts to real-world scenarios.

By mastering these advanced scripting techniques, you are now well-equipped to handle complex JSON data and optimize your PowerShell scripts for better performance. In the next chapter, we will explore real-world use cases and examples of JSON and PowerShell integration.

Chapter 8: Real-World Use Cases and Examples

Welcome to Chapter 8 of "PowerShell and JSON: From Beginner to Advanced." This chapter focuses on real-world use cases and practical examples of integrating JSON with PowerShell. You will explore scenarios such as configuration management, data transformation and migration, and automation of administrative tasks. These examples will help you understand how to apply the concepts you've learned in practical situations.

8.1 Configuration Management

Configuration management involves using JSON files to manage application and system settings. PowerShell can read, update, and generate configuration files, making it a powerful tool for managing configurations.

Key Points:

Configuration Files: JSON is a popular format for configuration files due to its readability and ease of use.

Reading and Updating Configurations: Use PowerShell to read, update, and write configuration settings in JSON format.

Practice:

1. Reading a Configuration File:

   - Create a sample configuration file named `config.json`:

   ```
   {
     "appSettings": {
         "appName": "MyApplication",
         "version": "1.0.0",
         "logging": {
             "level": "info",
             "path": "/var/log/myapp.log"
         }
     }
   }
   ```

   - Read the configuration file in PowerShell:

   ```
   $configPath = "config.json"
   $config = Get-Content -Path $configPath -Raw |
   ConvertFrom-Json
   $config.appSettings.appName
   $config.appSettings.logging.level
   ```

2. Updating a Configuration File:

   - Update the logging level and write the updated configuration back to the file:

   ```
   $config.appSettings.logging.level = "debug"
   $config | ConvertTo-Json -Depth 3 | Set-Content
   -Path $configPath
   ```

8.2 Data Transformation and Migration

Data transformation and migration involve converting data from one format to another and moving it between systems. PowerShell can transform data between JSON, CSV, and XML formats, and facilitate data migration.

Key Points:

Data Transformation: Convert data between JSON, CSV, and XML formats.

Data Migration: Move data between different systems using PowerShell scripts.

Practice:

1. Transform JSON to CSV:
   - Create a JSON file named `data.json`:

     ```
     [
         {"name": "Alice", "age": 28, "email":
     "alice@example.com"},
         {"name": "Bob", "age": 35, "email":
     "bob@example.com"}
     ]
     ```

   - Convert the JSON data to CSV:

     ```
     $jsonPath = "data.json"
     $jsonData = Get-Content -Path $jsonPath -Raw |
     ConvertFrom-Json
     $jsonData | Export-Csv -Path "data.csv"
     -NoTypeInformation
     ```

2. Transform CSV to JSON:

   - Create a CSV file named `data.csv`:

     ```
     name,age,email
     Alice,28,alice@example.com
     Bob,35,bob@example.com
     ```

   - Convert the CSV data to JSON:

     ```
     $csvPath = "data.csv"
     $csvData = Import-Csv -Path $csvPath
     $jsonString = $csvData | ConvertTo-Json
     $jsonString | Set-Content -Path
     "data_transformed.json"
     ```

3. Migrate Data Between Systems:

   - Fetch data from a web API and save it to a local file:

     ```
     $url = "https://jsonplaceholder.typicode.com/
     posts"
     $posts = Invoke-RestMethod -Uri $url -Method Get
     $posts | ConvertTo-Json -Depth 3 | Set-Content
     -Path "posts.json"
     ```

8.3 Scripting Automation with JSON

Automation with JSON involves using PowerShell scripts to automate repetitive tasks, such as generating reports, managing user accounts, and monitoring system performance.

Key Points:

Report Generation: Automate the creation of reports using JSON data.

User Account Management: Automate user account creation, updates, and deletions.

System Monitoring: Monitor system performance and generate alerts based on JSON data.

Practice:

1. Generate a Report from JSON Data:

   - Create a JSON file named `report_data.json`:

     ```
     [
        {"date": "2023-01-01", "sales": 100, "expenses": 50},
        {"date": "2023-01-02", "sales": 150, "expenses": 75}
     ]
     ```

   - Generate a sales report:

     ```
     $reportPath = "report_data.json"
     $reportData = Get-Content -Path $reportPath -Raw |
     ConvertFrom-Json
     foreach ($day in $reportData) {
        $profit = $day.sales - $day.expenses
        Write-Output "Date: $($day.date), Sales: $
     ($day.sales), Expenses: $($day.expenses), Profit:
     $profit"
     }
     ```

2. Automate User Account Management:

- Create a JSON file named `users.json`:

```json
[
  {"username": "alice", "password": "Password123!", "email": "alice@example.com"},
  {"username": "bob", "password": "Password456!", "email": "bob@example.com"}
]
```

- Automate user creation:

```powershell
$usersPath = "users.json"
$users = Get-Content -Path $usersPath -Raw |
ConvertFrom-Json
foreach ($user in $users) {
  New-LocalUser -Name $user.username -Password
(ConvertTo-SecureString $user.password
-AsPlainText -Force) -FullName $user.username
-Description $user.email
  Add-LocalGroupMember -Group "Users" -Member
$user.username
}
```

3. Monitor System Performance:

- Fetch system performance data and generate alerts:

```powershell
$cpuThreshold = 80
$memoryThreshold = 70
$systemData = @(
  @{
      "metric" = "CPU Usage"
      "value" = (Get-Counter '\Processor(_Total)\%
Processor Time').CounterSamples[0].CookedValue
  },
  @{
      "metric" = "Memory Usage"
      "value" = (Get-Counter '\Memory\% Committed
Bytes In Use').CounterSamples[0].CookedValue
  }
```

```
    )
    foreach ($metric in $systemData) {
        if ($metric.metric -eq "CPU Usage" -and
    $metric.value -gt $cpuThreshold) {
            Write-Output "Alert: $($metric.metric) is
    above threshold: $($metric.value)%"
        }
        if ($metric.metric -eq "Memory Usage" -and
    $metric.value -gt $memoryThreshold) {
            Write-Output "Alert: $($metric.metric) is
    above threshold: $($metric.value)%"
        }
    }
```

8.4 Practice Exercises

Exercise 1: Manage Application Configurations

Create a JSON configuration file for an application and write a PowerShell script to read and update a configuration setting.

```
{
    "application": {
        "name": "MyApp",
        "version": "1.0.0",
        "settings": {
            "theme": "light",
            "language": "en-US"
        }
    }
}


$configPath = "app_config.json"
```

```
$config = Get-Content -Path $configPath -Raw | ConvertFrom-Json
$config.application.settings.theme = "dark"
$config | ConvertTo-Json -Depth 3 | Set-Content -Path $configPath
```

Exercise 2: Transform and Migrate Data

Write a PowerShell script to transform user data from JSON to CSV and back to JSON, then migrate it to another system.

```
$jsonPath = "users.json"
$jsonData = Get-Content -Path $jsonPath -Raw | ConvertFrom-Json
$csvPath = "users.csv"
$jsonData | Export-Csv -Path $csvPath -NoTypeInformation
$csvData = Import-Csv -Path $csvPath
$jsonString = $csvData | ConvertTo-Json
$jsonString | Set-Content -Path "users_transformed.json"
```

Exercise 3: Automate Report Generation

Write a PowerShell script to generate a monthly sales report from JSON data.

```
$reportPath = "monthly_sales.json"
$reportData = Get-Content -Path $reportPath -Raw | ConvertFrom-Json
foreach ($day in $reportData) {
    $profit = $day.sales - $day.expenses
    Write-Output "Date: $($day.date), Sales: $($day.sales),
Expenses: $($day.expenses), Profit: $profit"
}
```

Exercise 4: Automate User Account Management

Write a PowerShell script to automate the creation of user accounts from JSON data.

```powershell
$usersPath = "new_users.json"
$users = Get-Content -Path $usersPath -Raw | ConvertFrom-Json
foreach ($user in $users) {
    New-LocalUser -Name $user.username -Password (ConvertTo-
SecureString $user.password -AsPlainText -Force) -FullName
$user.username -Description $user.email
    Add-LocalGroupMember -Group "Users" -Member $user.username
}
```

Exercise 5: Monitor and Alert System Performance

Write a PowerShell script to monitor CPU and memory usage and generate alerts if thresholds are exceeded.

```powershell
$cpuThreshold = 80
$memoryThreshold = 70
$systemData = @(
    @{
        "metric" = "CPU Usage"
        "value" = (Get-Counter '\Processor(_Total)\% Processor
Time').CounterSamples[0].CookedValue
    },
    @{
        "metric" = "Memory Usage"
        "value" = (Get-Counter '\Memory\% Committed Bytes In
Use').CounterSamples[0].CookedValue
    }
)
foreach ($metric in $systemData) {
    if ($metric.metric -eq "CPU Usage" -and $metric.value -gt
$cpuThreshold) {
```

```
        Write-Output "Alert: $($metric.metric) is above
threshold: $($metric.value)%"
    }
    if ($metric.metric -eq "Memory Usage" -and $metric.value -gt
$memoryThreshold) {
        Write-Output "Alert: $($metric.metric) is above
threshold: $($metric.value)%"
    }
}
```

Quiz

1. How can you read and update a JSON configuration file using Power-Shell?

```
# Read JSON file
$config = Get-Content -Path "config.json" | ConvertFrom-
Json

# Update a value
$config.setting1 = "new value"

# Add a new property
$config | Add-Member -MemberType NoteProperty -Name
"newSetting" -Value "value"

# Save updated JSON
$config | ConvertTo-Json | Set-Content -Path
"config.json"
```

2. Write a PowerShell script to convert JSON data to CSV and back to JSON.

```
# Read JSON file
$jsonData = Get-Content -Path "data.json" | ConvertFrom-
Json
```

```powershell
# Convert to CSV
$jsonData | Export-Csv -Path "data.csv"
-NoTypeInformation

# Read CSV back in
$csvData = Import-Csv -Path "data.csv"

# Convert back to JSON
$csvData | ConvertTo-Json | Set-Content -Path
"data_new.json"
```

3. How can you automate the creation of user accounts using JSON data in PowerShell?

```powershell
# Read JSON file with user data
$users = Get-Content -Path "users.json" | ConvertFrom-Json

foreach ($user in $users) {
    $params = @{
        Name = $user.username
        GivenName = $user.firstname
        Surname = $user.lastname
        AccountPassword = (ConvertTo-SecureString
$user.password -AsPlainText -Force)
        Enabled = $true
    }

    New-ADUser @params

    Write-Host "Created user: $($user.username)"
}
```

4. Write a PowerShell script to monitor system performance and generate alerts based on JSON data.

```powershell
# Read alert thresholds from JSON
$thresholds = Get-Content -Path "thresholds.json" | ConvertFrom-Json
```

```powershell
# Get current CPU and memory usage
$cpu = (Get-Counter '\Processor(_Total)\% Processor
Time').CounterSamples.CookedValue
$memory = (Get-Counter '\Memory\% Committed Bytes In
Use').CounterSamples.CookedValue

# Check against thresholds and generate alerts
if ($cpu -gt $thresholds.cpu) {
    Write-Host "ALERT: CPU usage is $cpu%, exceeding
threshold of $($thresholds.cpu)%"
}

if ($memory -gt $thresholds.memory) {
    Write-Host "ALERT: Memory usage is $memory%,
exceeding threshold of $($thresholds.memory)%"
}

# Log performance data to JSON
$perfData = @{
    timestamp = Get-Date -Format "yyyy-MM-dd HH:mm:ss"
    cpu = $cpu
    memory = $memory
}

$perfData | ConvertTo-Json | Add-Content -Path
"perflog.json"
```

These scripts demonstrate basic patterns for working with JSON in PowerShell. Remember to adjust file paths, property names, and specific commands as needed for your environment. Also, ensure you have the necessary permissions to perform these operations, especially for creating AD users or accessing system performance data.

In this chapter, you explored real-world use cases and practical examples of integrating JSON with PowerShell. You learned how to manage application configurations, transform and migrate data, and automate various tasks using PowerShell scripts. Practical exercises helped you apply these concepts to real-world scenarios.

By mastering these real-world use cases and examples, you are now well-equipped to handle practical scenarios involving JSON and PowerShell. In the next chapter, we will cover troubleshooting and best practices for working with JSON in PowerShell.

Chapter 9: Troubleshooting and Best Practices

Welcome to Chapter 9 of "PowerShell and JSON: From Beginner to Advanced." This chapter focuses on troubleshooting common issues and best practices for working with JSON in PowerShell. You will learn how to debug JSON-related errors, optimize your scripts for better performance, and follow best practices to write clean and maintainable code.

9.1 Debugging JSON in PowerShell

Debugging JSON in PowerShell involves identifying and resolving errors that occur when working with JSON data. Common issues include syntax errors, invalid data types, and unexpected data structures.

Key Points:

Syntax Errors: JSON must be properly formatted with correct use of commas, quotes, and braces.

Data Type Mismatches: Ensure JSON data types match the expected PowerShell types.

Unexpected Structures: Handle variations in JSON structure gracefully.

Practice:

1. Identify and Fix Syntax Errors:

    - Review the following JSON snippet and identify syntax errors:

    ```
    {
        "name": "Alice",
        "age": 28,
        "email": "alice@example.com"
        "active": true,
    }
    ```

    - Corrected JSON:

    ```
    {
        "name": "Alice",
        "age": 28,
        "email": "alice@example.com",
        "active": true
    }
    ```

    - Validate the corrected JSON using PowerShell:

    ```
    $jsonString = '{
        "name": "Alice",
        "age": 28,
        "email": "alice@example.com",
        "active": true
    }'
    $data = $jsonString | ConvertFrom-Json
    $data
    ```

2. Handle Data Type Mismatches:

    - Parse JSON with mismatched data types:

    ```
    $jsonString = '{
        "name": "Bob",
    ```

```
    "age": "thirty-five",
    "email": "bob@example.com",
    "active": "yes"
}'
try {
    $data = $jsonString | ConvertFrom-Json
} catch {
    Write-Error "Failed to parse JSON: $_"
}
```

- Correct the data types and re-parse:

```
$correctedJsonString = '{
    "name": "Bob",
    "age": 35,
    "email": "bob@example.com",
    "active": true
}'
$data = $correctedJsonString | ConvertFrom-Json
$data
```

3. Handle Unexpected Structures:

- Parse JSON with unexpected structures:

```
$jsonString = '{
    "users": [
    {"name": "Alice", "age": 28},
    {"name": "Bob", "age": 35}
    ],
    "metadata": {
    "total": 2,
    "success": true
    }
}'
$data = $jsonString | ConvertFrom-Json
$data.users
$data.metadata
```

9.2 Best Practices for JSON Handling

Following best practices for JSON handling ensures your PowerShell scripts are clean, efficient, and maintainable. This includes proper error handling, validating JSON data, and using efficient coding techniques.

Key Points:

Error Handling: Implement robust error handling to manage JSON parsing and conversion errors.

   Validation: Validate JSON data against schemas or expected structures.

   Efficiency: Optimize JSON processing for performance and resource usage.

Practice:

1. Implement Robust Error Handling:

    -   Use try-catch blocks to handle errors gracefully:

```
function Parse-Json {
  param (
      [string]$jsonString
  )
  try {
      return $jsonString | ConvertFrom-Json
  } catch {
      Write-Error "Error parsing JSON: $_"
  }
}
$jsonString = '{"name": "Alice", "age": 28}'
$data = Parse-Json -jsonString $jsonString
$data
```

2. Validate JSON Data:

  - Validate JSON data against a schema:

```
Install-Package Newtonsoft.Json.Schema

$schema = '{
  "$schema": "http://json-schema.org/draft-07/
schema#",
  "title": "User",
  "type": "object",
  "properties": {
      "name": { "type": "string" },
      "age": { "type": "integer" },
      "email": { "type": "string", "format":
"email" }
  },
  "required": ["name", "age"]
}'

$json = '{"name": "Alice", "age": 28, "email":
"alice@example.com"}'
$JSchema =
[Newtonsoft.Json.Schema.JSchema]::Parse($schema)
$JObject =
[Newtonsoft.Json.Linq.JObject]::Parse($json)
$isValid = $JObject.IsValid($JSchema)
$isValid
```

3. Optimize JSON Processing:

  - Use streaming techniques to handle large JSON files:

```
$filePath = "largeData.json"
$stream = [System.IO.StreamReader]::new($filePath)
while ($line = $stream.ReadLine()) {
  $jsonObject = $line | ConvertFrom-Json
  # Process each JSON object here
}
$stream.Close()
```

9.3 Security Considerations

When handling JSON data, it's essential to consider security aspects such as data validation, sanitization, and preventing injection attacks. Ensuring data integrity and confidentiality is critical in any application.

Key Points:

Input Validation: Validate all input data to prevent malicious data from being processed.

Sanitization: Remove or escape potentially harmful data.

Secure Transmission: Use HTTPS to encrypt data during transmission.

Practice:

1. Validate Input Data:

   - Use regular expressions or validation functions to ensure data meets expected formats:

```
function Validate-Email {
  param (
      [string]$email
  )
  if ($email -match '^[\w-\.]+@([\w-]+\.)+[\w-]
{2,4}$') {
      return $true
  } else {
      return $false
  }
}
$email = "test@example.com"
$isValidEmail = Validate-Email -email $email
$isValidEmail
```

2. Sanitize Input Data:

- Sanitize input data to remove or escape harmful characters:

```
function Sanitize-Input {
  param (
      [string]$input
  )
  $input = $input -replace '<', '&lt;'
  $input = $input -replace '>', '&gt;'
  $input = $input -replace '&', '&amp;'
  $input = $input -replace '"', '&quot;'
  $input = $input -replace "'", '&#39;'
  return $input
}
$input = "<script>alert('Hello')</script>"
$sanitizedInput = Sanitize-Input -input $input
$sanitizedInput
```

3. Ensure Secure Transmission:

- Use HTTPS to ensure data is encrypted during transmission:

```
$url = "https://secureapi.example.com/data"
$response = Invoke-RestMethod -Uri $url -Method
Get
$response
```

9.4 Practice Exercises

Exercise 1: Debug and Fix JSON Errors

Given a JSON string with syntax errors, debug and fix the errors:

```
{
   "title": "Book",
   "author": "John Doe"
   "pages": 300,
   "available": true,
}
```

```powershell
$jsonString = '{
   "title": "Book",
   "author": "John Doe",
   "pages": 300,
   "available": true
}'
$data = $jsonString | ConvertFrom-Json
$data
```

Exercise 2: Implement Error Handling in a PowerShell Function

Write a PowerShell function to parse JSON and handle errors gracefully:

```powershell
function Parse-Json {
    param (
        [string]$jsonString
    )
    try {
        return $jsonString | ConvertFrom-Json
```

```
    } catch {
        Write-Error "Error parsing JSON: $_"
    }
}
$jsonString = '{"name": "Alice", "age": 28}'
$data = Parse-Json -jsonString $jsonString
$data
```

Exercise 3: Validate JSON Data Against a Schema

Create a JSON schema for a product object and validate JSON data against it:

```
$schema = '{
    "$schema": "http://json-schema.org/draft-07/schema#",
    "title": "Product",
    "type": "object",
    "properties": {
        "name": { "type": "string" },
        "price": { "type": "number" },
        "in_stock": { "type": "boolean" }
    },
    "required": ["name", "price"]
}'

$json = '{"name": "Laptop", "price": 999.99, "in_stock": true}'
$JSchema = [Newtonsoft.Json.Schema.JSchema]::Parse($schema)
$JObject = [Newtonsoft.Json.Linq.JObject]::Parse($json)
$isValid = $JObject.IsValid($JSchema)
$isValid
```

Exercise 4: Optimize Processing of Large JSON Files

Write a PowerShell script to efficiently process a large JSON file using streaming:

```
$filePath = "largeData.json"
$stream = [System.IO.StreamReader]::new($filePath)
while ($line = $stream.ReadLine()) {
    $jsonObject = $line | ConvertFrom-Json
    # Process each JSON object here
}
$stream.Close()
```

Exercise 5: Sanitize User Input Data

Write a PowerShell function to sanitize user input to prevent injection attacks:

```
function Sanitize-Input {
    param (
        [string]$input
    )
    $input = $input -replace '<', '&lt;'
    $input = $input -replace '>', '&gt;'
    $input = $input -replace '&', '&amp;'
    $input = $input -replace '"', '&quot;'
    $input = $input -replace "'", '&#39;'
    return $input
}
$input = "<script>alert('Hello')</script>"
$sanitizedInput = Sanitize-Input -input $input
$sanitizedInput
```

Quiz

1. What are common JSON syntax errors, and how can you fix them?

   Common JSON syntax errors include:

   - Missing or extra commas

- Unmatched brackets or braces

- Using single quotes instead of double quotes

- Trailing commas in arrays or objects

- Missing colons between keys and values

To fix these:

- Ensure all commas are correctly placed

- Check that all brackets and braces are properly matched

- Use only double quotes for strings

- Remove trailing commas

- Add colons between keys and values

2. Write a PowerShell function to handle JSON parsing errors gracefully.

```powershell
function Parse-JsonSafely {
    param (
        [Parameter(Mandatory=$true)]
        [string]$JsonString
    )

    try {
        $parsedJson = $JsonString | ConvertFrom-Json
        return $parsedJson
    }
    catch [System.ArgumentException] {
        Write-Error "Invalid JSON string: $
($_.Exception.Message)"
    }
    catch {
        Write-Error "An unexpected error occurred: $
($_.Exception.Message)"
    }
}
```

3. How can you validate JSON data against a schema in PowerShell?

To validate JSON against a schema in PowerShell, you can use the `Test-Json` cmdlet (available in PowerShell 6.0 and later) or a third-party module like `Pester-Schema`.

Using `Test-Json`:

```
$schema = @'
{
   "type": "object",
   "properties": {
       "name": { "type": "string" },
       "age": { "type": "integer" }
   },
   "required": ["name", "age"]
}
'@

$json = '{"name": "John", "age": 30}'

if (Test-Json -Json $json -Schema $schema) {
   Write-Output "JSON is valid"
} else {
   Write-Output "JSON is invalid"
}
```

4. Write a PowerShell script to efficiently process a large JSON file.

```
$filePath = "C:\path\to\large\file.json"
$outputPath = "C:\path\to\output.txt"

# Read the file in chunks
$reader = [System.IO.File]::OpenText($filePath)
$jsonContent = ""
$buffer = New-Object char[] 8192
$processedCount = 0

while ($reader.Read($buffer, 0, $buffer.Length) -gt 0) {
   $jsonContent += $buffer

   # Process complete JSON objects
   while ($jsonContent -match '(\{[^{}]*\})') {
```

```
        $match = $matches[1]
        $jsonObject = $match | ConvertFrom-Json

        # Process the JSON object (example: write to
output file)
        $jsonObject | Select-Object -Property Name, Age |
Out-File -Append $outputPath

        $jsonContent =
$jsonContent.Substring($jsonContent.IndexOf($match) +
$match.Length)
        $processedCount++
    }
}

$reader.Close()
Write-Output "Processed $processedCount JSON objects"
```

5. How can you sanitize user input data to prevent injection attacks?

   To sanitize user input and prevent injection attacks:

   - Use parameterized queries or prepared statements when work-
     ing with databases.

   - Validate and sanitize input data before processing:

```
function Sanitize-Input {
    param (
        [Parameter(Mandatory=$true)]
        [string]$Input
    )

    # Remove potentially harmful characters
    $sanitized = $Input -replace '[<>&''"()]', ''

    # Encode HTML entities
    $sanitized =
[System.Web.HttpUtility]::HtmlEncode($sanitized)

    # Trim whitespace
    $sanitized = $sanitized.Trim()
```

```
    return $sanitized
}

# Usage
$userInput = Read-Host "Enter some text"
$safeInput = Sanitize-Input -Input $userInput
```

- Use the principle of least privilege when executing commands or scripts.

- Implement input validation using regular expressions to ensure the input matches expected patterns:

```
function Validate-Input {
   param (
        [Parameter(Mandatory=$true)]
        [string]$Input,
        [Parameter(Mandatory=$true)]
        [string]$Pattern
   )

   if ($Input -match $Pattern) {
        return $true
   } else {
        return $false
   }
}

# Usage
$userInput = Read-Host "Enter a username
(alphanumeric, 3-20 characters)"
$isValid = Validate-Input -Input $userInput
-Pattern "^[a-zA-Z0-9]{3,20}$"

if ($isValid) {
   Write-Output "Valid input"
} else {
   Write-Output "Invalid input"
}
```

In this chapter, you learned how to troubleshoot common issues and follow best practices for working with JSON in PowerShell. You explored techniques for debugging JSON errors, validating and sanitizing JSON data, and optimizing JSON processing for better performance. Practical exercises helped you apply these concepts to real-world scenarios.

By mastering these troubleshooting techniques and best practices, you are now well-equipped to handle any challenges that arise when working with JSON in PowerShell. Congratulations on completing the course!

Appendices

The appendices provide additional resources, references, and example scripts to support your learning journey. They serve as a quick reference guide and offer practical tools and tips to enhance your PowerShell and JSON skills.

Appendix A: PowerShell Cmdlet Reference

This appendix provides a comprehensive reference for essential PowerShell cmdlets used throughout the book. It includes descriptions, syntax, and examples for each cmdlet.

Key Cmdlets:

- Get-Command: Lists all available cmdlets and functions.

   ```
   Get-Command
   ```

- Get-Help: Provides detailed help information for cmdlets.

   ```
   Get-Help Get-Process
   ```

- ConvertFrom-Json: Converts a JSON-formatted string to a PowerShell object.

```
$jsonString = '{"name": "John", "age": 30}'
$object = $jsonString | ConvertFrom-Json
```

- ConvertTo-Json: Converts a PowerShell object to a JSON-formatted string.

```
$object = @{name="John"; age=30}
$jsonString = $object | ConvertTo-Json
```

- Invoke-RestMethod: Sends an HTTP request to a web API and processes the response.

```
$url = "https://jsonplaceholder.typicode.com/posts/1"
$response = Invoke-RestMethod -Uri $url -Method Get
```

Appendix B: JSON Schema Reference

This appendix provides a reference for JSON Schema, including the basic structure, data types, and validation rules. It helps you understand how to define and validate JSON data using schemas.

Key Points:

Basic Structure:

```
{
    "$schema": "http://json-schema.org/draft-07/schema#",
    "title": "Example Schema",
    "type": "object",
    "properties": {
        "propertyName": {
```

```
            "type": "dataType"
        }
    },
    "required": ["propertyName"]
}
```

Data Types:

String: "type": "string"

Number: "type": "number"

Integer: "type": "integer"

Boolean: "type": "boolean"

Array: "type": "array"

Object: "type": "object"

Null: "type": "null"

Practice:

1. Create a JSON Schema:

```
{
    "$schema": "http://json-schema.org/draft-07/schema#",
    "title": "Product Schema",
    "type": "object",
    "properties": {
        "name": {
            "type": "string"
        },
        "price": {
            "type": "number"
        },
        "in_stock": {
            "type": "boolean"
        }
    },
    "required": ["name", "price"]
```

```
}
```

Appendix C: Example Scripts and Code Snippets

This appendix provides a collection of example scripts and code snippets to help you apply the concepts learned in the book. These examples cover common tasks such as parsing JSON, sending HTTP requests, and automating administrative tasks.

Examples:

1. Parse and Display JSON Data:

```
$jsonString = '{"name": "John", "age": 30, "email":
"john@example.com"}'
$data = $jsonString | ConvertFrom-Json
Write-Output "Name: $($data.name)"
Write-Output "Age: $($data.age)"
Write-Output "Email: $($data.email)"
```

2. Send a POST Request with JSON Data:

```
$url = "https://jsonplaceholder.typicode.com/posts"
$body = @{
    title = "foo"
    body = "bar"
    userId = 1
} | ConvertTo-Json
$response = Invoke-RestMethod -Uri $url -Method Post
-Body $body -ContentType "application/json"
```

```powershell
$response
```

3. Automate User Account Creation:

```powershell
$users = @(
    @{username="alice"; password="Password123!";
email="alice@example.com"},
    @{username="bob"; password="Password456!";
email="bob@example.com"}
)
foreach ($user in $users) {
    New-LocalUser -Name $user.username -Password
(ConvertTo-SecureString $user.password -AsPlainText
-Force) -FullName $user.username -Description
$user.email
    Add-LocalGroupMember -Group "Users" -Member
$user.username
}
```

4. Monitor System Performance and Generate Alerts:

```powershell
$cpuThreshold = 80
$memoryThreshold = 70
$systemData = @(
    @{
        "metric" = "CPU Usage"
        "value" = (Get-Counter '\Processor(_Total)\%
Processor Time').CounterSamples[0].CookedValue
    },
    @{
        "metric" = "Memory Usage"
        "value" = (Get-Counter '\Memory\% Committed Bytes
In Use').CounterSamples[0].CookedValue
    }
)
foreach ($metric in $systemData) {
    if ($metric.metric -eq "CPU Usage" -and $metric.value
-gt $cpuThreshold) {
        Write-Output "Alert: $($metric.metric) is above
threshold: $($metric.value)%"
```

```
    }
    if ($metric.metric -eq "Memory Usage" -and
$metric.value -gt $memoryThreshold) {
        Write-Output "Alert: $($metric.metric) is above
threshold: $($metric.value)%"
    }
}
```

PowerShell Glossary

A

Active Directory (AD)

A directory service developed by Microsoft for Windows domain networks, providing a variety of network services, including LDAP-like directory access and authentication services.

Alias

A shorthand name for a cmdlet or command. Aliases make it easier to use frequently used commands. For example, `ls` is an alias for `Get-ChildItem`. They are useful for shortening long cmdlets for quick access.

Array

A data structure that stores a collection of elements, accessible by index. Arrays can contain elements of different data types and are commonly used to store lists of items. They are essential for handling multiple pieces of data in a single variable.

Argument

A value that is passed to a function, script, or cmdlet to provide input data. Arguments are typically provided after a parameter name in the command line and help customize the behavior of commands.

ArgumentList

A parameter in the Invoke-Command cmdlet that allows you to pass arguments to the script block being executed on a remote computer.

Attribute

A piece of metadata added to a cmdlet, function, or parameter to specify behavior or characteristics. Attributes can control how parameters are processed, provide validation, and more, enhancing the functionality and robustness of scripts.

API (Application Programming Interface)

A set of rules and protocols for building and interacting with software applications, allowing different systems to communicate with each other.

B

Boolean

A data type that can hold one of two values: $true or $false. Booleans are typically used in conditional statements to control the flow of execution and make decisions in scripts.

Break

A keyword used to exit a loop or switch statement prematurely. It is useful for stopping the execution flow based on certain conditions, such as when a desired value is found.

Breakpoint

A debugging tool that pauses script execution at a specified line, allowing the user to inspect the current state of the script.

Background Job

A task that runs asynchronously in the background. Background jobs allow you to perform long-running operations without blocking the main PowerShell session, enabling multitasking and efficient resource use.

Basic Authentication

An authentication method that transmits credentials in an unencrypted form. It is recommended to use it only over secure connections (HTTPS).

C

Cmdlet

A lightweight command used in the PowerShell environment, typically following a verb-noun naming convention (e.g., `Get-Process`). Cmdlets perform specific operations and return objects, making them powerful tools for automation and management.

Comment

Text in a script that is not executed, used for documentation. Single-line comments start with #, while multi-line comments are enclosed in <# #>. Comments are essential for explaining code and making scripts easier to understand, aiding in maintenance and collaboration.

Credential

An object that contains a user's username and password. Credentials are used to authenticate users and access secure resources, ensuring security and proper access control.

Configuration

A declarative PowerShell script used to define the desired state of an environment, typically used in Desired State Configuration (DSC). Configurations help maintain consistency across multiple systems by automating setup and enforcement of settings.

CredSSP (Credential Security Support Provider)

An authentication method that allows delegation of user credentials from the client to the target server for multi-hop authentication scenarios.

Custom Session Configuration

A session configuration that defines specific settings and constraints for remote sessions, such as which cmdlets and modules are available.

CSV (Comma-Separated Values)

A file format used to store tabular data, where each line is a data record, and each record consists of fields separated by commas.

D

Data Transformation

The process of converting data from one format or structure to another.

Dynamic Object

An object in PowerShell that can have properties and methods added or removed at runtime.

DSC (Desired State Configuration)

A management platform in PowerShell that enables you to manage your IT and development infrastructure with configuration as code. DSC ensures that the components of a system are in a desired state, providing a reliable and repeatable way to deploy and manage configurations.

Data Type

A classification that specifies the type of data a variable can hold, such as integer, string, boolean, array, or object. Understanding data types is crucial for handling and manipulating data correctly in PowerShell scripts.

Debug

A process of identifying and removing errors from software. PowerShell provides cmdlets and tools for debugging scripts and modules, helping developers find and fix issues efficiently.

Debugging

The process of identifying and removing errors from computer hardware or software.

E

Execution Policy

A security feature that determines which PowerShell scripts can be run on a system. Common policies include Restricted, AllSigned, RemoteSigned, and Unrestricted. Execution policies help protect systems from running malicious scripts by controlling script execution.

Export-Csv

A cmdlet that converts objects into CSV (comma-separated values) format and writes them to a file. This is useful for exporting data in a format that can be easily imported into other applications, like Excel, facilitating data sharing and analysis.

Exception

An error that occurs during the execution of a script or command. PowerShell provides mechanisms for handling exceptions using `try`, `catch`, and `finally` blocks, allowing scripts to handle errors gracefully and continue execution.

Error Handling

The process of responding to and managing errors that occur during script execution.

Enable-PSRemoting

A cmdlet that configures a computer to receive PowerShell remote commands.

Enter-PSSession

A cmdlet that starts an interactive session with a remote computer.

Exit-PSSession

A cmdlet that ends an interactive session with a remote computer.

F

ForEach-Object

A cmdlet that processes each item in a collection of input objects. It is commonly used to perform actions on each item in a pipeline, enabling efficient processing of data streams.

Function

A named block of reusable code that performs a specific task. Functions can accept parameters and return values, making them useful for modularizing code and improving reusability, thereby enhancing script organization and maintainability.

Format-Table

A cmdlet that formats the output as a table with the selected properties of the object displayed in columns. It improves the readability of output data by organizing it into a structured format.

G

GET

An HTTP method used to request data from a specified resource.

Get-Command

A cmdlet that retrieves all commands that are available in your session. This includes cmdlets, functions, aliases, and scripts, helping users discover available commands and their functionalities.

Get-Help

A cmdlet that provides detailed information about PowerShell commands and concepts. It is essential for understanding how to use different cmdlets and functions, offering syntax, parameters, and examples.

Get-Process

A cmdlet that retrieves information about processes running on a local or remote computer. It is commonly used for process monitoring and management, providing insights into system performance and application behavior.

Global Variable

A variable that is accessible from anywhere within the PowerShell session. Global variables are defined using the $global: scope modifier, allowing data to be shared across different parts of a script or session.

GUI (Graphical User Interface)

A visual way of interacting with a computer using items like windows, icons, and menus, used in contrast to a command-line interface.

H

Hash Table

A data structure that stores key-value pairs. Hash tables are used for quick data retrieval based on keys and are useful for storing configuration settings and other related data, offering efficient look-up operations.

Host

The application that is hosting the PowerShell runtime. This could be the Power-Shell console, ISE, or another application that embeds the PowerShell engine, providing the environment in which scripts and commands are executed.

Hyper-V

A virtualization platform by Microsoft that allows you to create and manage virtual machines. PowerShell provides cmdlets for managing Hyper-V environments, enabling automation of virtualization tasks.

HTTP (Hypertext Transfer Protocol)

The protocol used for transferring data over the web, which defines methods such as GET, POST, PUT, and DELETE.

HTTPS (Hypertext Transfer Protocol Secure)

An extension of HTTP that is used for secure communication over a computer network within a web browser.

I

ISE (Integrated Scripting Environment)

A graphical interface for writing, testing, and debugging PowerShell scripts. The ISE provides features such as syntax highlighting, debugging tools, and a built-in console, enhancing the scripting experience and productivity.

IDE (Integrated Development Environment)

A software suite that combines common developer tools into a single graphical user interface (GUI), such as Visual Studio Code for PowerShell scripting.

Import-Csv

A cmdlet that reads a CSV file and converts it into a collection of objects. This is useful for importing data from CSV files into PowerShell for processing, facilitating data manipulation and analysis.

Invoke-Command

A cmdlet that runs commands on local and remote computers. It is commonly used for executing scripts and cmdlets on multiple machines simultaneously, enabling centralized management and automation.

Import-Module

A cmdlet that loads a PowerShell module into the current session, making its cmdlets, functions, and other resources available for use. Modules help organize and distribute reusable scripts and functions.

Implicit Remoting

A technique where cmdlets from a remote session are imported into the local session, allowing you to run remote cmdlets as if they were local.

Integer

A data type in JSON representing whole numbers without a fractional component.

Invoke-Command

A cmdlet used to run commands on one or more remote computers.

Invoke-RestMethod

A PowerShell cmdlet used to send HTTP and HTTPS requests to RESTful web services and handle their responses.

J

Job

A background task that runs asynchronously. Jobs are useful for performing long-running operations without blocking the main PowerShell session, allowing for efficient multitasking and resource management.

Join-Path

A cmdlet that combines a path and child path into a single path. This is useful for constructing file and directory paths, ensuring correct and portable path formats.

Just Enough Administration (JEA)

A security technology that enables you to create constrained PowerShell endpoints where users have limited administrative privileges.

JSON (JavaScript Object Notation)

A lightweight data interchange format that is easy for humans to read and write, and easy for machines to parse and generate.

JSON Schema

A vocabulary that allows you to annotate and validate JSON documents, defining the structure and constraints of JSON data.

L

Loop

A control structure that repeats a block of code a specified number of times or while a condition is true. Common loop types in PowerShell include `for`, `foreach`, `while`, and `do-while`, enabling repetitive operations and iteration over collections.

Logging

The process of recording information about the execution of a script. Logging can include details such as start and end times, errors, and significant events, aiding in troubleshooting and auditing.

M

Module

A package containing PowerShell commands, providers, functions, variables, and other types of resources that can be imported as a unit. Modules help organize and distribute PowerShell scripts and functions, enhancing reusability and maintainability.

Multi-line Comment

A comment that spans multiple lines, enclosed in <# and #>. Multi-line comments are useful for providing detailed explanations or documenting large sections of code, improving code readability and understanding.

Measure-Object

A cmdlet that calculates the numeric properties of objects, such as count, average, sum, minimum, and maximum values. It is useful for statistical analysis and summarizing data.

Method

A function associated with an object in programming, defining behavior or actions that the object can perform.

MIME Type

A standard way of indicating the nature and format of a file or data stream, often used in HTTP headers to specify the content type.

N

Namespace

A container that holds a set of related classes, interfaces, and other types. Namespaces help organize code and prevent naming conflicts, enabling modular development and code reuse.

Nested Function

A function defined within another function. Nested functions can access the variables and parameters of their parent function, allowing for encapsulation and modular code organization.

Null

A data type in JSON representing an empty or non-existent value, denoted as null.

O

Object

An instance of a class that contains data and methods. In PowerShell, everything is an object, including numbers, strings, and cmdlet outputs, providing a consistent way to interact with data and commands.

Out-File

A cmdlet that sends output to a file. This is useful for saving the results of a command or script to a text file, enabling persistent storage and later analysis.

Object-Oriented Programming (OOP)

A programming paradigm based on the concept of "objects", which can contain data and code to manipulate the data.

Optimization

The process of improving the efficiency of a script or program to reduce execution time and resource usage.

P

Parsing

The process of analyzing a string or data structure and converting it into a usable format, such as converting a JSON string into a PowerShell object.

Parameter

A variable that is passed to a function, script, or cmdlet. Parameters allow you to pass data and control the behavior of scripts and functions, enhancing flexibility and reusability.

Pipeline

A series of commands connected by the pipe operator (|), where the output of one command becomes the input of the next. Pipelines allow for powerful data processing and transformation, enabling complex workflows to be built from simple commands.

PowerShell Core

The open-source, cross-platform version of PowerShell. PowerShell Core runs on Windows, macOS, and Linux, and is based on .NET Core, providing a consistent scripting environment across different operating systems.

Provider

An interface that allows access to data and components that are not typically part of the file system, such as the registry, certificate store, and environment variables. Providers enable PowerShell to interact with a wide range of data stores using a common set of cmdlets.

Parallel Execution

Running multiple commands or scripts simultaneously to improve efficiency and performance.

PSSession (PowerShell Session)

A persistent connection to a remote computer that allows you to run multiple commands without re-establishing the connection each time.

POST

An HTTP method used to send data to a server to create or update a resource.

Q

Query

The process of requesting data from a database or other data source. PowerShell can be used to query databases using cmdlets and modules designed for database access, enabling data retrieval and manipulation.

R

Remoting

The ability to run commands on one or more remote computers. PowerShell remoting is essential for managing multiple systems and performing administrative tasks remotely, facilitating centralized control and automation.

Remote Computer

A computer that is accessed and managed using PowerShell Remoting.

Repository

A centralized location where PowerShell modules and scripts can be stored and shared. PowerShell Gallery is a popular public repository for PowerShell content, promoting code reuse and collaboration.

Runspace

An instance of the PowerShell execution environment. Runspaces allow you to run multiple PowerShell commands simultaneously in separate threads, enabling parallel processing and efficient resource utilization.

REST (Representational State Transfer)

An architectural style for designing networked applications, using stateless communication and standard HTTP methods.

S

Sanitization

The process of removing or escaping potentially harmful data to prevent security vulnerabilities, such as injection attacks.

Schema

A structured framework or blueprint that defines the organization, format, and constraints of data.

Script

A file containing a series of PowerShell commands that can be executed as a unit. Scripts are used to automate tasks and perform complex operations, enhancing productivity and consistency.

Script Block

A collection of statements or expressions that can be used as a single unit. Script blocks are used in many PowerShell constructs, such as functions, filters, and workflows, providing a flexible way to group code.

Script Block Logging

A logging feature that records the content of all script blocks that are executed.

Secure String

A type of string that is encrypted in memory to protect sensitive information, such as passwords. Secure strings are used to enhance security in scripts, ensuring that sensitive data is not exposed in plain text.

Switch Statement

A control structure that executes one block of code among many based on the value of a variable or expression. Switch statements provide a clear and efficient way to handle multiple conditions.

Session Configuration File

A file that defines the settings and constraints for a remote PowerShell session.

SSH (Secure Shell)

A protocol for secure remote login and other secure network services over an insecure network.

SSL/TLS (Secure Sockets Layer/Transport Layer Security)

Cryptographic protocols designed to provide secure communication over a computer network.

String

A sequence of characters used to represent text.

Streaming

A technique for processing large data sets in chunks, rather than loading the entire data set into memory at once.

T

Transcript

A record of all commands and output from a PowerShell session, created using the `Start-Transcript` cmdlet. Transcripts are useful for auditing and troubleshooting, providing a detailed log of script execution.

Try, Catch, Finally

Keywords used to handle exceptions in PowerShell scripts. `Try` contains the code that may produce an error, `Catch` handles the error, and `Finally` executes code regardless of whether an error occurred, ensuring proper cleanup and resource management.

Type Accelerator

A shortcut for creating instances of .NET classes in PowerShell. Type accelerators make it easier to work with .NET objects, providing a more concise syntax for commonly used types.

Throttle Limit

A parameter that controls the number of simultaneous connections when running commands on multiple remote computers using Invoke-Command.

U

Unblock-File

A cmdlet that removes the "blocked" status from a file downloaded from the internet, allowing it to be executed without restrictions. This is useful for handling files that Windows marks as potentially unsafe.

Update-Help

A cmdlet that downloads and installs the latest help files for PowerShell modules from the internet. Keeping help files up to date ensures access to the most current documentation and usage information.

Using Scope Modifier

A keyword used to pass local variables to remote sessions within a script block.

URL (Uniform Resource Locator)

The address used to access a specific resource on the web.

V

Variable

A storage location that holds a value. In PowerShell, variables start with $. Variables can store data of any type and are used to pass information between commands and scripts, enabling dynamic and flexible script behavior.

Validation

The process of checking that data conforms to expected formats, structures, and constraints, ensuring data integrity and consistency.

Verbose

A common parameter that provides detailed information about the actions being performed by a cmdlet. The -Verbose switch is used to enable verbose output, aiding in debugging and understanding script execution.

Virtual Machine

A software-based emulation of a physical computer. PowerShell can be used to create, configure, and manage virtual machines, especially in Hyper-V and VMware environments, facilitating virtualization and testing.

W

Windows PowerShell

The original Windows-only version of PowerShell, based on the .NET Framework. It is different from PowerShell Core, which is cross-platform, and provides extensive capabilities for managing Windows systems.

Workflow

A sequence of programmed, connected steps that perform long-running tasks or require coordination of multiple steps across multiple devices. Workflows are used to automate complex processes, ensuring reliable and repeatable execution.

WMI (Windows Management Instrumentation)

A set of specifications from Microsoft for consolidating the management of devices and applications in a network. PowerShell can use WMI to query system information and manage Windows components, providing powerful system management capabilities.

WinRM (Windows Remote Management)

A Microsoft implementation of the WS-Management protocol that allows hardware and operating systems from different vendors to interoperate.

WSMan (Web Services for Management)

A standard protocol used for remote management of computer systems.

Where-Object

A PowerShell cmdlet used to filter objects in the pipeline based on specified conditions.

X

XML

A markup language used for encoding documents in a format that is both human-readable and machine-readable. PowerShell can work with XML data using cmdlets like `ConvertTo-Xml` and `Select-Xml`, enabling structured data processing and manipulation.

XPath

A language used for selecting nodes from an XML document. PowerShell can use XPath to query XML data, providing precise control over data extraction and manipulation.

Z

ZipFile

A class in the .NET Framework used to create, extract, and manage ZIP archive files. PowerShell can interact with ZIP files using this class for compression and extraction tasks, facilitating file management and storage.

JSON Command Table for PowerShell

Command	Description	Syntax	Example
ConvertFrom-Json	Converts a JSON-formatted string to a PowerShell object.	ConvertFrom-Json -InputObject <jsonString>	`$jsonString = '{"name": "John", "age": 30}' $object = $jsonString | ConvertFrom-Json $object
ConvertTo-Json	Converts a PowerShell object to a JSON-formatted string.	ConvertTo-Json -InputObject <object> [-Depth <depth>] [-Compress]	$object = @{name="John"; age=30} $jsonString = $object | ConvertTo-Json $jsonString
Invoke-Rest-Method	Sends an HTTP request to a web API and processes the JSON response.	Invoke-Rest-Method -Uri <url> -Method <method> [-Body <body>] [-ContentType <contentType>]	$url = "https://json-placeholder.-typicode.com/posts/1" $response = Invoke-Rest-Method -Uri $url -Method Get $response

Get-Content	Reads the content of a file, which can include JSON data.	Get-Content -Path <file-Path> [-Raw]	$jsonString = Get-Content -Path "data.json" -Raw $jsonData = $jsonString | ConvertFrom-Json $jsonData
Set-Content	Writes data to a file, which can include JSON-formatted strings.	Set-Content -Path <file-Path> -Value <data>	$jsonString = $data | ConvertTo-Json $jsonString | Set-Content -Path "data.json"
Add-Member	Adds properties to an object, useful for modifying JSON objects.	Add-Member -InputObject <object> -MemberType <memberType> -Name <name> -Value <value>	$object = [PSCustomObject]@{name="John"; age=30} $object | Add-Member -MemberType NoteProperty -Name "email" -Value "john@example.com"
Remove-Member	Removes properties from an object, useful for modifying JSON objects.	Remove-Member -InputObject <object> -Name <name>	$object = [PSCustomObject]@{name="John"; age=30; email="john@example.com"} $object | Remove-Member -Name "email"

Import-Csv	Converts CSV data into PowerShell objects, which can then be converted to JSON.	Import-Csv -Path <file-Path>	$csvData = Import-Csv -Path "data.csv" $jsonData = $csvData | ConvertTo-Json $jsonData
Export-Csv	Converts PowerShell objects into CSV format and writes them to a file.	Export-Csv -Path <file-Path> -NoType-Information	$jsonData = '[{"name":"John","age":30}, {"name":"Jane","age":25}]' $data = $jsonData | Convert-From-Json $data | Export-Csv -Path "data.csv" -NoTypeInformation

Examples

1. Convert JSON String to PowerShell Object

```
$jsonString = '{"name": "Alice", "age": 28, "email": "alice@example.com"}'
$data = $jsonString | ConvertFrom-Json
Write-Output "Name: $($data.name)"
Write-Output "Age: $($data.age)"
Write-Output "Email: $($data.email)"
```

2. Convert PowerShell Object to JSON String

```powershell
$object = @{
   name = "Bob"
   age = 35
   email = "bob@example.com"
}
$jsonString = $object | ConvertTo-Json -Depth 3
$jsonString
```

3. Send a POST Request with JSON Data

```powershell
$url = "https://jsonplaceholder.typicode.com/posts"
$body = @{
   title = "foo"
   body = "bar"
   userId = 1
} | ConvertTo-Json
$response = Invoke-RestMethod -Uri $url -Method Post
-Body $body -ContentType "application/json"
$response
```

4. Read JSON Data from a File

```powershell
$jsonString = Get-Content -Path "data.json" -Raw
$data = $jsonString | ConvertFrom-Json
$data
```

5. Write JSON Data to a File

```powershell
$object = @{
   name = "Charlie"
   age = 40
   email = "charlie@example.com"
}
$jsonString = $object | ConvertTo-Json -Depth 3
$jsonString | Set-Content -Path "output.json"
```

6. Add a Property to a JSON Object

```
$object = [PSCustomObject]@{name="Dave"; age=45}
$object | Add-Member -MemberType NoteProperty -Name
"email" -Value "dave@example.com"
$object
```

7. Remove a Property from a JSON Object

```
$object = [PSCustomObject]@{name="Eve"; age=50;
email="eve@example.com"}
$object | Remove-Member -Name "email"
$object
```

8. Convert CSV to JSON

```
$csvData = Import-Csv -Path "data.csv"
$jsonData = $csvData | ConvertTo-Json
$jsonData
```

9. Convert JSON to CSV

```
$jsonString = '[{"name":"Frank","age":60},
{"name":"Grace","age":55}]'
$data = $jsonString | ConvertFrom-Json
$data | Export-Csv -Path "output.csv" -NoTypeInformation
```

JSON Quick Reference

This JSON Quick Reference provides a concise guide to the essential elements, syntax, and usage of JSON. It includes common data types, structures, formatting rules, and practical examples to help you work effectively with JSON data.

JSON Data Types

Data Type	Description	Example
String	A sequence of characters	`"hello"`
Number	An integer or floating-point number	`123`, `45.67`
Object	A collection of key/value pairs	`{"key": "value"}`
Array	An ordered list of values	`["value1", "value2"]`
Boolean	A true or false value	`true`, `false`
Null	An empty value	`null`

JSON Object Example

Description: A JSON object representing a person, including nested objects and arrays.

```
{
    "name": "Alice",
    "age": 28,
    "email": "alice@example.com",
    "isActive": true,
```

```
    "address": {
        "street": "123 Main St",
        "city": "Anytown",
        "zip": "12345"
    },
    "phoneNumbers": [
        "555-1234",
        "555-5678"
    ]
}
```

JSON Array Example

Description: A JSON array containing multiple objects.

```
[
    {
        "name": "John",
        "age": 30
    },
    {
        "name": "Jane",
        "age": 25
    },
    {
        "name": "Jim",
        "age": 35
    }
]
```

Nested JSON Example

Description: A JSON object containing a nested object and a nested array.

```
{
```

```
    "user": {
        "id": 1,
        "name": "Alice",
        "roles": ["admin", "user"],
        "settings": {
            "theme": "dark",
            "notifications": true
        }
    }
}
```

JSON Formatting Tips

1. Indentation: Use spaces or tabs to indent JSON data for readability.

```
{
    "name": "John",
    "age": 30
}
```

2. Consistent Quotes: Use double quotes "" for all keys and string values.

```
{
    "key": "value"
}
```

3. Trailing Commas: Do not include a comma after the last key/value pair or array item.

```
{
    "name": "John",
    "age": 30
}
```

Common JSON Operations in Power-Shell

1. Convert JSON String to PowerShell Object:

```
$jsonString = '{"name": "Alice", "age": 28}'
$object = $jsonString | ConvertFrom-Json
```

2. Convert PowerShell Object to JSON String:

```
$object = @{name = "Bob"; age = 35}
$jsonString = $object | ConvertTo-Json
```

3. Read JSON Data from a File:

```
$jsonString = Get-Content -Path "data.json" -Raw
$data = $jsonString | ConvertFrom-Json
```

4. Write JSON Data to a File:

```
$object = @{name = "Charlie"; age = 40}
$jsonString = $object | ConvertTo-Json -Depth 3
$jsonString | Set-Content -Path "output.json"
```

JSON Reference Table

JSON Element Description		Syntax/Example
Object	A collection of key/value pairs, enclosed in curly braces { }.	`{ "key": "value", "key2": "value2" }`
Array	An ordered list of values, enclosed in square brackets [].	`[ "value1", "value2", "value3" ]`
String	A sequence of characters, enclosed in double quotes "".	`"string value"`
Number	A numeric value, which can be an integer or floating-point.	`123, 45.67`
Boolean	A logical value, either `true` or `false`.	`true, false`
Null	A null value, representing no value.	`null`
Key	A string representing the name in a key/value pair, enclosed in double quotes "".	`"key": "value"`
Value	The value in a key/value pair, which can be any JSON data type.	`"key": "value", "key": 123, "key": true, "key": null, "key": [1, 2, 3], "key": { "nestedKey": "value" }`
Nested Object	An object within another object.	`{ "key": { "nestedKey": "nestedValue" } }`
Nested Array	An array within another array or object.	`{ "key": [ { "nestedKey": "nestedValue" }, { "nestedKey2": "nestedValue2" } ] }`

Examples

JSON Object

Description: A collection of key/value pairs, enclosed in curly braces { }.

```
{
    "name": "Alice",
    "age": 28,
    "email": "alice@example.com",
    "isActive": true,
    "address": {
        "street": "123 Main St",
        "city": "Anytown",
        "zip": "12345"
    },
    "phoneNumbers": [
        "555-1234",
        "555-5678"
    ]
}
```

JSON Array

Description: An ordered list of values, enclosed in square brackets [ ].

```
[
    {
        "name": "John",
        "age": 30
    },
    {
        "name": "Jane",
        "age": 25
    },
    {
        "name": "Jim",
        "age": 35
    }
]
```

JSON String

Description: A sequence of characters, enclosed in double quotes "".

```
{
    "message": "Hello, World!"
}
```

JSON Number

Description: A numeric value, which can be an integer or floating-point.

```
{
    "integer": 123,
    "float": 45.67
}
```

JSON Boolean

Description: A logical value, either true or false.

```
{
    "isAdmin": true,
    "isGuest": false
}
```

JSON Null

Description: A null value, representing no value.

```
{
    "middleName": null
}
```

Nested JSON Object

Description: An object within another object.

```json
{
    "user": {
        "name": "Alice",
        "profile": {
            "age": 28,
            "email": "alice@example.com"
        }
    }
}
```

Nested JSON Array

Description: An array within another array or object.

```json
{
    "library": {
        "books": [
            {
                "title": "Book 1",
                "author": "Author 1"
            },
            {
                "title": "Book 2",
                "author": "Author 2"
            }
        ]
    }
}
```

JSON Syntax Rules

1. Data is in name/value pairs: Each pair is separated by a colon : and enclosed in double quotes "".

   ```json
   { "name": "Alice" }
   ```

2. Data is separated by commas: Each key/value pair is separated by a comma `,`.

```
{ "name": "Alice", "age": 28 }
```

3. Curly braces hold objects: Objects are enclosed in curly braces `{}`.

```
{ "user": { "name": "Alice", "age": 28 } }
```

4. Square brackets hold arrays: Arrays are enclosed in square brackets `[]`.

```
{ "names": ["Alice", "Bob", "Charlie"] }
```

5. Keys must be strings: Keys are always strings, enclosed in double quotes `""`.

```
{ "key": "value" }
```

6. Values can be strings, numbers, objects, arrays, booleans, or null: Values can be various data types.

```
{
    "string": "text",
    "number": 123,
    "object": { "key": "value" },
    "array": [1, 2, 3],
    "boolean": true,
    "null": null
}
```

This table and the detailed examples provide a quick reference to essential JSON elements and their syntax, helping you efficiently work with JSON data in your PowerShell scripts and other applications.

JSON Templates

Here are several JSON templates that you can use as a reference for different scenarios such as configuration files, data records, API payloads, and more.

1. Configuration File Template

Description:

A template for an application configuration file, which includes settings for the application name, version, logging, and database connection.

```json
{
    "appSettings": {
        "appName": "MyApplication",
        "version": "1.0.0",
        "logging": {
            "level": "info",
            "path": "/var/log/myapp.log"
        }
    },
    "database": {
        "host": "localhost",
        "port": 5432,
        "username": "dbuser",
        "password": "password",
        "databaseName": "myappdb"
    },
    "features": {
        "enableFeatureX": true,
        "enableFeatureY": false
    }
}
```

2. User Data Template

Description:

A template for user data records, including personal information, contact details, and account settings.

```
{
    "user": {
        "userId": "12345",
        "name": "John Doe",
        "age": 30,
        "email": "john.doe@example.com",
        "phoneNumbers": [
            "555-1234",
            "555-5678"
        ],
        "address": {
            "street": "123 Main St",
            "city": "Anytown",
            "state": "CA",
            "zip": "12345"
        },
        "account": {
            "username": "johndoe",
            "password": "securepassword",
            "createdDate": "2024-01-01T12:00:00Z",
            "roles": ["user", "admin"]
        }
    }
}
```

3. Product Inventory Template

Description:

A template for a product inventory system, including details about products, their categories, and stock levels.

```json
{
    "products": [
        {
            "productId": "P001",
            "productName": "Product 1",
            "category": "Category A",
            "price": 19.99,
            "inStock": true,
            "stockQuantity": 100,
            "tags": ["tag1", "tag2"]
        },
        {
            "productId": "P002",
            "productName": "Product 2",
            "category": "Category B",
            "price": 29.99,
            "inStock": false,
            "stockQuantity": 0,
            "tags": ["tag3", "tag4"]
        }
    ]
}
```

4. API Request Payload Template

Description:

A template for an API request payload, including necessary parameters for creating a new user account.

```json
{
    "createUserRequest": {
        "username": "newuser",
        "password": "newpassword",
        "email": "newuser@example.com",
        "profile": {
            "firstName": "New",
            "lastName": "User",
            "birthDate": "1990-01-01",
            "gender": "male"
        },
        "preferences": {
            "language": "en",
            "timezone": "UTC-5"
        }
    }
}
```

5. API Response Template

Description:

A template for an API response payload, including the status of the request and details about the created user account.

```json
{
    "status": "success",
    "message": "User account created successfully",
    "data": {
        "userId": "67890",
        "username": "newuser",
        "email": "newuser@example.com",
        "profile": {
            "firstName": "New",
            "lastName": "User",
            "birthDate": "1990-01-01",
            "gender": "male"
```

```
        },
        "createdDate": "2024-07-28T15:00:00Z"
    }
}
```

6. Logging Configuration Template

Description:

A template for logging configuration, specifying log levels, output destinations, and log rotation settings.

```
{
    "logging": {
        "level": "debug",
        "output": {
            "console": true,
            "file": {
                "enabled": true,
                "path": "/var/log/myapp.log",
                "maxSizeMB": 100,
                "maxFiles": 10
            }
        },
        "rotation": {
            "enabled": true,
            "frequency": "daily"
        }
    }
}
```

7. E-Commerce Order Template

Description:

A template for an e-commerce order, including customer details, items purchased, and payment information.

```json
{
    "order": {
        "orderId": "ORD12345",
        "orderDate": "2024-07-28T14:00:00Z",
        "customer": {
            "customerId": "CUST123",
            "name": "Alice Johnson",
            "email": "alice.johnson@example.com",
            "phone": "555-1234"
        },
        "items": [
            {
                "itemId": "ITEM001",
                "productName": "Product 1",
                "quantity": 2,
                "price": 19.99
            },
            {
                "itemId": "ITEM002",
                "productName": "Product 2",
                "quantity": 1,
                "price": 29.99
            }
        ],
        "totalAmount": 69.97,
        "payment": {
            "method": "credit_card",
            "transactionId": "TXN12345",
            "status": "completed"
        },
        "shipping": {
            "address": {
                "street": "456 Elm St",
                "city": "Othertown",
```

```
                "state": "NY",
                "zip": "67890"
            },
            "method": "standard",
            "status": "shipped",
            "trackingNumber": "TRACK12345"
        }
    }
}
```

These JSON templates can serve as starting points for various scenarios in your projects. Customize them according to your specific needs and use them to streamline your JSON data handling in PowerShell and other programming environments.

JSONLint

Introduction to JSONLint

Objective:

Understand what JSONLint is, why it is useful, and how to access it.

Key Points:

1. What is JSONLint?

   - JSONLint is an online tool used to validate and format JSON (JavaScript Object Notation) data.

   - It helps identify and correct syntax errors in JSON data.

   - Provides a formatted, human-readable version of JSON data.

2. Why Use JSONLint?

   - Ensures JSON data is correctly formatted and adheres to JSON standards.

   - Helps in debugging JSON-related issues in applications.

   - Makes JSON data more readable and easier to manage.

3. Accessing JSONLint:

   - JSONLint can be accessed through the web at JSONLint.

   - No installation is required; it is an entirely web-based tool.

Understanding JSONLint Features

Objective:

Explore the main features of JSONLint and understand how to use them.

Key Points:

1. Validate JSON:

   - JSONLint checks the syntax of JSON data to ensure it is valid.

   - It identifies errors such as missing commas, unmatched brackets, and incorrect use of quotes.

2. Format JSON:

   - JSONLint formats JSON data to make it more readable.

   - It adds indentation and line breaks for better clarity.

3. Error Messages:

   - JSONLint provides detailed error messages to help you understand and fix issues.

   - Error messages indicate the line number and type of error.

Practice:

1. Validating JSON Data:

   - Open JSONLint in your web browser.

   - Paste the following JSON data into the text area:

   ```
   {
       "name": "John Doe",
       "age": 30
   ```

```
    "email": "john.doe@example.com"
}
```

- Click the "Validate JSON" button.
- Observe the error message indicating a missing comma after the "age" property.

2. Formatting JSON Data:
   - Paste the following unformatted JSON data into JSONLint:

```
{"name":"Jane
Doe","age":25,"email":"jane.doe@example.com"}
```

   - Click the "Validate JSON" button.
   - Observe the formatted JSON output.

Using JSONLint for Debugging

Objective:

Learn how to use JSONLint to debug and correct common JSON errors.

Key Points:

1. Common JSON Errors:
   - Missing or extra commas.
   - Unmatched brackets or braces.
   - Incorrect use of quotes (single vs. double).
   - Missing property names or values.

2. Debugging Process:

    - Paste the JSON data into JSONLint.

    - Click the "Validate JSON" button.

    - Review the error messages and locate the issues.

    - Correct the errors in the JSON data.

    - Validate again until the JSON is error-free.

Practice:

1. Debugging Missing Comma:

    - Paste the following JSON data into JSONLint:

    ```
    {
        "name": "Alice",
        "age": 28
        "email": "alice@example.com"
    }
    ```

    - Click the "Validate JSON" button.

    - Correct the missing comma after the "age" property and vali-
       date again.

2. Debugging Unmatched Brackets:

    - Paste the following JSON data into JSONLint:

    ```
    {
        "name": "Bob",
        "age": 35,
        "email": "bob@example.com"
    ```

    - Click the "Validate JSON" button.

- Add the missing closing brace } and validate again.

3. Debugging Incorrect Quotes:
    - Paste the following JSON data into JSONLint:

    ```
    {
      "name": "Charlie",
      "age": 40,
      "email": 'charlie@example.com'
    }
    ```

    - Click the "Validate JSON" button.
    - Change the single quotes around the email value to double quotes and validate again.

Advanced Features of JSONLint

Objective:

Explore advanced features of JSONLint, such as schema validation and custom configurations.

Key Points:

1. Schema Validation:
    - JSONLint supports validating JSON data against a schema.
    - This ensures that JSON data adheres to a specific structure and data types.

2. Custom Configurations:

- JSONLint allows custom configuration for validation and formatting.
- Users can specify settings such as indentation size and error display options.

Practice:

Schema Validation:

- Define a JSON schema for user data:

```
{
    "$schema": "http://json-schema.org/draft-07/
schema#",
    "title": "User",
    "type": "object",
    "properties": {
        "name": {
            "type": "string"
        },
        "age": {
            "type": "integer"
        },
        "email": {
            "type": "string",
            "format": "email"
        }
    },
    "required": ["name", "age", "email"]
}
```

- Paste the schema and the following JSON data into JSONLint:

```
{
    "name": "Eve",
    "age": "twenty-five",
```

```
        "email": "eve@example.com"
    }
```

- Click the "Validate JSON" button.
- Observe the schema validation error indicating that the age property should be an integer.

Custom Configuration:

- Experiment with different settings in JSONLint, such as changing the indentation size.
    - Validate and format the following JSON data to see the effects:

```
{"name":"David","age":50,"email":"david@example.com"}
```

Best Practices for JSONLint

Objective:

Learn best practices for using JSONLint effectively in your projects.

Key Points:

1. **Regular Validation**:
    - Regularly validate your JSON data during development to catch errors early.
    - Use JSONLint to ensure data integrity and consistency.
2. **Consistent Formatting**:

- Use JSONLint to maintain consistent formatting across your JSON data.
- This improves readability and maintainability.

3. **Integration with Development Workflow**:

- Integrate JSONLint into your development workflow for automated validation.
    - Use JSONLint as part of your code review and quality assurance processes.

Practice:

1. Regular Validation:
    - Set a reminder to validate JSON data regularly in your projects.
    - Use JSONLint to validate the following JSON data:

```
{
    "project": "JSONLint Integration",
    "status": "ongoing",
    "team": [
        {"name": "Alice", "role": "developer"},
        {"name": "Bob", "role": "tester"}
    ]
}
```

2. Consistent Formatting:
    - Format the above JSON data using JSONLint to ensure it is consistently styled.
3. Integration with Workflow:
    - Explore ways to integrate JSONLint with your text editor or IDE.

- Look for plugins or extensions that support JSONLint for real-time validation.

Summary

Objective:

Review the key points and ensure you are ready to apply what you have learned.

Key Points:

- JSONLint is a powerful tool for validating and formatting JSON data.
- It helps identify and correct syntax errors, making JSON data more readable.
- Use JSONLint regularly to maintain data integrity and consistency.
- Explore advanced features such as schema validation and custom configurations.
- Integrate JSONLint into your development workflow for better quality assurance.

Practice:

- Regularly validate your JSON data using JSONLint.
- Use JSONLint to format your JSON data for improved readability.
- Experiment with schema validation and custom configurations.

- Integrate JSONLint into your development workflow for automated validation.

By mastering the use of JSONLint, you can ensure your JSON data is always valid, well-formatted, and consistent, making your projects more reliable and maintainable.

PowerShell Verbs Table

Verb	Description	Example Cmdlets
Add	Adds a resource to a container or another resource.	`Add-Content`, `Add-Member`
Clear	Removes all the items from a container.	`Clear-Content`, `Clear-Variable`
Close	Closes a resource.	`Close-EventLog`
Copy	Copies a resource to a new location.	`Copy-Item`, `Copy-ItemProperty`
Enter	Sets the current location to the specified resource.	`Enter-PSSession`
Exit	Exits a resource.	`Exit-PSSession`
Find	Finds a resource in a container.	`Find-Module`
Format	Formats a resource for output.	`Format-Table`, `Format-List`
Get	Retrieves data or information from a resource.	`Get-Process`, `Get-Content`
Invoke	Performs an operation on a resource.	`Invoke-Command`, `Invoke-RestMethod`
Join	Joins resources.	`Join-Path`
Lock	Locks a resource.	`Lock-BitLocker`
Move	Moves a resource to a new location.	`Move-Item`, `Move-ItemProperty`
New	Creates a new resource.	`New-Item`, `New-Object`
Open	Opens a resource.	`Open-EventLog`
Remove	Removes a resource from a container.	`Remove-Item`, `Remove-Variable`
Rename	Changes the name of a resource.	`Rename-Item`, `Rename-Computer`

Reset	Resets a resource to its original state.	`Reset-Computer`
Set	Modifies or configures a resource.	`Set-Content`, `Set-Location`
Start	Initiates an operation or resource.	`Start-Process`, `Start-Service`
Stop	Stops an operation or resource.	`Stop-Process`, `Stop-Service`
Suspend	Temporarily halts an operation or resource.	`Suspend-Service`
Unlock	Unlocks a resource.	`Unlock-BitLocker`
Update	Modifies an existing resource to reflect new information.	`Update-Help`, `Update-Module`
Use	Uses a resource.	`Use-Transaction`
Write	Writes data to a resource.	`Write-Output`, `Write-Host`

Project

This project aims to provide a comprehensive, hands-on experience with JSON and PowerShell. You will create a simple project that involves managing an employee database. The project will cover creating, reading, updating, and deleting (CRUD) operations using JSON data and PowerShell scripts. By the end of this project, you will have a better understanding of how to work with JSON data in a real-world scenario.

Project Overview

Objective:

Create a PowerShell-based application to manage an employee database stored in a JSON file. The application will support CRUD operations and provide a simple command-line interface for interacting with the database.

Components:

1. Employee JSON Schema
2. PowerShell Scripts for CRUD Operations
3. User Interface Script

Step 1: Define the Employee JSON Schema

Description:

Create a JSON schema to define the structure of the employee data.

Employee JSON Schema:

```json
{
    "$schema": "http://json-schema.org/draft-07/schema#",
    "title": "Employee",
    "type": "object",
    "properties": {
        "id": {
            "type": "string"
        },
        "firstName": {
            "type": "string"
        },
        "lastName": {
            "type": "string"
        },
        "email": {
            "type": "string",
            "format": "email"
        },
        "phone": {
            "type": "string"
        },
        "position": {
            "type": "string"
        },
        "department": {
            "type": "string"
        }
    },
    "required": ["id", "firstName", "lastName", "email",
"position", "department"]
}
```

Step 2: Create the Employee Database File

Description:

Create an initial JSON file to store employee data.

Initial JSON File (employees.json):

```json
[
    {
        "id": "1",
        "firstName": "Alice",
        "lastName": "Johnson",
        "email": "alice.johnson@example.com",
        "phone": "555-1234",
        "position": "Developer",
        "department": "IT"
    },
    {
        "id": "2",
        "firstName": "Bob",
        "lastName": "Smith",
        "email": "bob.smith@example.com",
        "phone": "555-5678",
        "position": "Manager",
        "department": "HR"
    }
]
```

Step 3: PowerShell Script for CRUD Operations

Description:

Create PowerShell functions to perform CRUD operations on the employee database.

CRUD Operations Script (EmployeeCRUD.ps1):

```powershell
# Load Employee Data
function Load-Employees {
    param (
        [string]$filePath
    )
```

```powershell
    if (Test-Path -Path $filePath) {
        $jsonString = Get-Content -Path $filePath -Raw
        return $jsonString | ConvertFrom-Json
    } else {
        return @()
    }
}

# Save Employee Data
function Save-Employees {
    param (
        [array]$employees,
        [string]$filePath
    )
    $jsonString = $employees | ConvertTo-Json -Depth 3
    $jsonString | Set-Content -Path $filePath
}

# Add Employee
function Add-Employee {
    param (
        [array]$employees,
        [hashtable]$newEmployee
    )
    $employees += [PSCustomObject]$newEmployee
    return $employees
}

# Get Employee by ID
function Get-EmployeeById {
    param (
        [array]$employees,
        [string]$employeeId
    )
    return $employees | Where-Object { $_.id -eq $employeeId }
}

# Update Employee
function Update-Employee {
    param (
        [array]$employees,
        [hashtable]$updatedEmployee
```

```powershell
    )
    for ($i = 0; $i -lt $employees.Count; $i++) {
        if ($employees[$i].id -eq $updatedEmployee.id) {
            $employees[$i] = [PSCustomObject]$updatedEmployee
            break
        }
    }
    return $employees
}

# Remove Employee
function Remove-Employee {
    param (
        [array]$employees,
        [string]$employeeId
    )
    return $employees | Where-Object { $_.id -ne $employeeId }
}

# Sample usage
# $employees = Load-Employees -filePath "employees.json"
# $employees = Add-Employee -employees $employees -newEmployee @{
#     id = "3"
#     firstName = "Laszlo"
#     lastName = "Bocso"
#     email = "bocso.laszlo@bosco-it.hu"
#     phone = "555-9876"
#     position = "Trainer"
#     department = "Education"
# }
# Save-Employees -employees $employees -filePath "employees.json"
```

Step 4: Create the User Interface Script

Description:

Create a PowerShell script to provide a simple command-line interface for interacting with the employee database.

User Interface Script (EmployeeUI.ps1):

```powershell
# Import CRUD Functions
. .\EmployeeCRUD.ps1

# File path to the employee database
$filePath = "employees.json"

# Load Employees
$employees = Load-Employees -filePath $filePath

function Show-Menu {
    Write-Host "Employee Management System"
    Write-Host "1. View All Employees"
    Write-Host "2. Add New Employee"
    Write-Host "3. Update Employee"
    Write-Host "4. Remove Employee"
    Write-Host "5. Exit"
}

function View-AllEmployees {
    Write-Host "ID  First Name  Last Name  Email  Phone  Position  Department"
    foreach ($employee in $employees) {
        Write-Host "$($employee.id)  $($employee.firstName)  $($employee.lastName)  $($employee.email)  $($employee.phone)  $($employee.position)  $($employee.department)"
    }
}

function Add-NewEmployee {
    $newEmployee = @{
        id = (Read-Host "Enter ID")
        firstName = (Read-Host "Enter First Name")
        lastName = (Read-Host "Enter Last Name")
        email = (Read-Host "Enter Email")
        phone = (Read-Host "Enter Phone")
        position = (Read-Host "Enter Position")
```

```powershell
        department = (Read-Host "Enter Department")
    }
    $employees = Add-Employee -employees $employees -newEmployee
$newEmployee
    Save-Employees -employees $employees -filePath $filePath
    Write-Host "Employee added successfully."
}


function Update-ExistingEmployee {
    $employeeId = Read-Host "Enter the ID of the employee to
update"
    $employee = Get-EmployeeById -employees $employees
-employeeId $employeeId
    if ($employee) {
        $updatedEmployee = @{
            id = $employee.id
            firstName = (Read-Host "Enter First Name" -Default
$employee.firstName)
            lastName = (Read-Host "Enter Last Name" -Default
$employee.lastName)
            email = (Read-Host "Enter Email" -Default
$employee.email)
            phone = (Read-Host "Enter Phone" -Default
$employee.phone)
            position = (Read-Host "Enter Position" -Default
$employee.position)
            department = (Read-Host "Enter Department" -Default
$employee.department)
        }
        $employees = Update-Employee -employees $employees
-updatedEmployee $updatedEmployee
        Save-Employees -employees $employees -filePath $filePath
        Write-Host "Employee updated successfully."
    } else {
        Write-Host "Employee not found."
    }
}


function Remove-ExistingEmployee {
    $employeeId = Read-Host "Enter the ID of the employee to
remove"
```

```
        $employee = Get-EmployeeById -employees $employees
-employeeId $employeeId
    if ($employee) {
        $employees = Remove-Employee -employees $employees
-employeeId $employeeId
        Save-Employees -employees $employees -filePath $filePath
        Write-Host "Employee removed successfully."
    } else {
        Write-Host "Employee not found."
    }
}

# Main Program Loop
while ($true) {
    Show-Menu
    $choice = Read-Host "Enter your choice"
    switch ($choice) {
        1 { View-AllEmployees }
        2 { Add-NewEmployee }
        3 { Update-ExistingEmployee }
        4 { Remove-ExistingEmployee }
        5 { break }
        default { Write-Host "Invalid choice. Please try
again." }
    }
    Write-Host ""
}

Write-Host "Exiting Employee Management System."
```

By completing this project, you have gained practical experience with JSON and PowerShell. You have learned how to:

- Define and use a JSON schema for structured data.
- Implement CRUD operations using PowerShell scripts.
- Create a command-line interface for interacting with a JSON-based database.

- Extend and enhance the functionality of your scripts to handle real-world requirements.

This project has equipped you with the skills needed to manage JSON data effectively and automate tasks using PowerShell.

Summary

This book, "PowerShell and JSON: From Beginner to Advanced," provides a comprehensive guide to mastering the use of JSON within PowerShell. Throughout the chapters, you have learned the essential concepts, practical applications, and advanced techniques needed to work effectively with JSON data in PowerShell. Here's a summary of what you have covered:

Chapter 1: Introduction to PowerShell and JSON

- PowerShell Basics: Overview of PowerShell, installation, and basic commands.
- JSON Fundamentals: Introduction to JSON, its structure, and its importance in data interchange.

Chapter 2: Getting Started with PowerShell

- Installation and Basic Commands: Step-by-step instructions to install PowerShell on different platforms and run basic commands.
- PowerShell Scripting: Introduction to writing and running PowerShell scripts.

Chapter 3: Understanding JSON Syntax

- JSON Data Types: Strings, numbers, objects, arrays, booleans, and null.
- JSON Structure: Key/value pairs, nested objects, and arrays.
- Common JSON Formatting Issues: Identifying and correcting JSON syntax errors.

Chapter 4: Working with JSON in PowerShell

- Parsing JSON: Converting JSON strings to PowerShell objects using ConvertFrom-Json.
- Creating JSON: Generating JSON strings from PowerShell objects using ConvertTo-Json.
- Modifying JSON Data: Accessing and updating properties of JSON objects.

Chapter 5: Advanced JSON Manipulation

- Complex JSON Structures: Working with nested objects and arrays.
- Filtering JSON Data: Using Where-Object to filter JSON data based on conditions.
- Merging and Combining JSON Data: Integrating multiple JSON objects or arrays.

Chapter 6: Integrating JSON with External Services

- Consuming Web APIs: Sending HTTP requests to APIs and handling JSON responses using Invoke-RestMethod.
- Automating API Interactions: Creating reusable functions and handling errors in API interactions.
- Storing and Retrieving JSON Data: Saving JSON responses to files and reading JSON data from files.

Chapter 7: Advanced PowerShell Scripting with JSON

- Creating JSON Schemas: Defining and validating JSON structures using schemas.
- Dynamic JSON Processing: Handling JSON data with unknown structures using dynamic objects.
- Performance Optimization: Efficient parsing and generation of JSON, memory management.

Chapter 8: Real-World Use Cases and Examples

- Configuration Management: Managing application settings using JSON configuration files.
- Data Transformation and Migration: Converting data between JSON, CSV, and XML formats.

- Scripting Automation with JSON: Automating tasks like report generation, user account management, and system monitoring.

Chapter 9: Troubleshooting and Best Practices

- Debugging JSON in PowerShell: Identifying and resolving JSON-related errors.
- Best Practices for JSON Handling: Implementing error handling, validation, and efficient coding techniques.
- Security Considerations: Validating and sanitizing JSON data, ensuring secure transmission.

Appendices

- PowerShell Cmdlet Reference: A comprehensive list of essential PowerShell cmdlets with syntax and examples.
- JSON Schema Reference: Guidelines for creating and validating JSON schemas.
- Common JSON Tools and Libraries: Tools and libraries for working with JSON in various programming languages.
- Example Scripts and Code Snippets: Practical examples to help you apply the concepts learned.

Glossary

A glossary of terms to enhance your understanding of PowerShell, JSON, and related technologies.

JSON Reference Table

A quick reference guide for JSON elements, including syntax, examples, and descriptions.

Made in the USA
Las Vegas, NV
09 March 2025

19285199R10105